Praise for
Leading for Results

In this inventive "self-help" handbook for educators, Dennis Sparks, the voice of professional development in our field, offers a compelling message: the power to lead and to learn resides within each of us if we will only summon it forth and live by it. He challenges—and helps us—not to do something different but to BE something different.

Roland S. Barth
Author and Educator

Sparks rejects simplistic solutions to school improvement. He honors the craft knowledge and expertise of educators and contends that "teacher-to-teacher communication about teaching and learning is the most powerful and sustained source of professional learning and instructional improvement." Like many of the leading contemporary educational thinkers, Sparks defines the challenge facing school leaders as "the development of a high performance culture" based on collaboration, continuous improvement and positive, powerful relationships built on trust. Unlike most others, however, he offers a wealth of information on what schools can do to build such cultures and relationships. The book serves as a powerful catalyst for dialogue, and I concur with Sparks's conclusion that its "value will best be realized by a study group whose members are committed to improving professional learning, teaching, and leadership in their schools." His powerful ideas and specific suggestions will give readers a lot to digest.

Richard DuFour
Educational Author and Consultant

Leading for Results is brimming with useful insights and practices for teachers, principals, superintendents and all leaders who wish to transform educational organizations. Dennis Sparks identifies easy-to-use and long-lasting skills from the wisdom of scholars and practitioners. His approach is pragmatic and based on well-reasoned assumptions about the heart and practice of professional learning. Leaders wishing to transform educational institutions need look no further than this helpful book.

Jane Dutton
*William Russell Kelly Professor
of Business Administration
University of Michigan Business School*

Dennis Sparks's Leading for Results *consists of 26 gems of action-oriented vignettes. Each is a treasure in its own right, and together they make up a consistent and powerful call to action. A powerful book of purposeful reform for those at all levels of the system committed to getting results.*

Michael Fullan
Professor, University of Toronto

This book is a statement of vision and potential practices based on the deepest principles of school—and human—development. The author's hopeful theme is that leaders (teachers and others) can overcome resignation and dependency as they move groups toward possibility and personal power. More than a recipe on leadership, Sparks poses personal assumptions on each topic and challenges readers to examine their own. The content is easily accessible and congruent with today's best thinking about school improvement.

Robert Garmston
*Professor Emeritus
California State University, Sacramento*

In Leading for Results, *Dennis Sparks invites readers to take part in a journey of self-discovery and actualization. In this highly personalized description of his own transformation as an educational leader, Sparks carves a path through the dense jungle of organizational complexity, helping others to see their own paths to effective leadership in new and clearer ways. He offers not only a compelling vision of what true leadership can be, but also describes specific steps on how to get there. It's a fascinating journey, incredibly worthwhile, and never more important than today.*

Thomas R. Guskey
Professor, University of Kentucky

This book is a good read, but it is intended to be used as well as read. In fact, the author provides specific instructions regarding ways to use this book. Almost certainly, those who use this book as the author intends will find it worth the effort. It is also likely that many readers will learn much that they need to know about themselves, about leadership, and about results. I know I did.

By writing this book, the author has done a real favor for all of us who want to improve education. I hope it will be widely used.

Phillip Schlechty
CEO, Schlechty Center for Leadership in School Reform

In Leading For Results, *Dennis Sparks has given us a practical, original and tough-minded book abut what schools need now. Each succinct, provocative section helps us to see that in order to survive—to thrive—schools must possess candor and courage and take smart, deliberate action. An excellent book—but even more, a book to act on.*

Mike Schmoker
Consultant and Author

LEADING
FOR RESULTS

LEADING
FOR RESULTS

Transforming Teaching, Learning,
and Relationships in Schools

DENNIS SPARKS

Roberta —
With warm
regards —
Dennis

A JOINT PUBLICATION

CORWIN PRESS
A Sage Publications Company
Thousand Oaks, California

NATIONAL ASSOCIATION
OF SECONDARY SCHOOL
PRINCIPALS

For information:

Corwin Press
A Sage Publications Company
2455 Teller Road
Thousand Oaks, California 91320
www.corwinpress.com

Sage Publications Ltd
1 Oliver's Yard
55 City Road
London EC1Y 1SP
United Kingdom

Sage Publications India Pvt. Ltd.
B-42, Panchsheel Enclave
Post Box 4109
New Delhi 110 017 India

Printed in the United States of America

Library of Congress Cataloging-in-Publication Data

Sparks, Dennis.
Leading for results : transforming teaching, learning, and relationships in schools / Dennis Sparks.
    p. cm.
Includes bibliographical references and index.
ISBN 1-4129-1392-6 (cloth) — ISBN 1-4129-1393-4 (pbk.)
    1. School management and organization. 2. Educational leadership. I. Title.

LB2805.S735 2005
371.2—dc22

                                    2004019866

This book is printed on acid-free paper.

05   06   07   08   09   10   9   8   7   6   5   4   3   2

NSDC Editor	Joan Richardson
Acquisitions Editor:	Rachel Livsey
Editorial Assistant:	Phyllis Cappello
Production Editor:	Sanford Robinson
Copy Editor:	Melissa Messina
Typesetter:	C&M Digitals (P) Ltd.
Proofreader:	Eileen Delaney
Cover Designer:	Terry Taylor
Indexer:	Teri Greenberg

Contents

Introduction

CHANGE OURSELVES TO CHANGE ORGANIZATIONS

[E]very day of your life is filled with opportunities to be creative, to act with purpose and potency. You don't need an elevated position or a title of great importance to assume a leadership role.

—Larraine Matusak

One who sees the invisible can do the impossible.

—Frank Gaines

Leaders matter. What leaders think, say, and do—and who they are when they come to work each day—profoundly affects organizational performance, the satisfaction they and those with whom they interact derive from their work, and their ability to sustain engagement with their work over the period of time necessary to oversee significant improvements. Leaders' thoughts and actions shape the culture of their organizations and set the direction and pace for the professional learning that is essential in improving organizational performance.

Significant change in organizations begins, therefore, with significant change in what leaders think, say, and do. *Leading for Results: Transforming Teaching, Learning, and Relationships in Schools* offers my view on the nature of these changes and how they can be initiated, deepened over time, and used to produce changes in teaching and relationships that benefit all students. Underneath this view, of course, is my belief that the knowledge, skills, and attitudes described in this book can be developed and nurtured through both formal and informal means.

The type of leadership discussed here might be labeled transformational or authentic. Transformational leadership has as its goal fundamental changes in individuals, organizations, and society. Authentic leadership flows from self-awareness regarding intentions, values, and feelings and wields its influence through actions congruent with that self-awareness. Both transformational and authentic leadership are founded on the belief that individuals can have a profound influence on one another and their organization through particular kinds of interactions and creative processes. Such leadership may be provided by both an organization's official leaders and others within the organization who apply the beliefs and skills presented in these pages.

The type of leadership I advocate activates latent potential within organizations and energizes those who live and work within them. It promotes extraordinary performance in otherwise "ordinary" people. These ideas will be developed throughout the book.

An Inner Departure

In *The Cultural Creatives: How 50 Million People Are Changing the World*, Paul Ray and Sherry Ruth Anderson (2000) describe the "inner departures" or turning points that shape our lives. They write: "Whether your inner departure is sparked by something you saw on TV or in the morning paper, or by a personal shock and loss; whether it started in childhood or in the middle of your life or at retirement—at some point, the previously accepted explanation of how things came to be the way they are doesn't satisfy you anymore" (p. 48).

Over a number of years, I came to realize that my work to improve the quality of teacher and administrator professional learning for the benefit of students was not producing the results I desired. During those years, I had talked with thousands of educators in countless settings about the importance of high-quality professional learning and the nature of the professional development that led to that learning. I would present research findings, quote experts, provide practical tips on how to do those things, answer questions, and ask participants to discuss what they were learning and to set goals.

I gradually came to see that this approach was not working, but I did not know another way to create the results I desired. So I lived for several years in an uncomfortable in-between state convinced that what I was doing wasn't working while feeling frustrated and rudderless because I did not know of another way.

Over time, with the assistance of many people, I began to develop the ideas I present in this book. I offer these ideas to you not as "truth," but as an invitation to explore them with an open mind and a sense of possibility that they may lead you to the things you most value and want in your school and life. I hope that you will give each of these ideas careful examination and a thoughtful appraisal as you experiment with them in whatever settings seem most appropriate.

Make the Invisible Visible

I believe deeply in the importance of actualizing human ability and of the critical role that organizational leaders play in both the development and full use of that potential. Before it is actualized, though, that potential is invisible. It lies latent, unnoticed, waiting to be manifested.

Likewise, the human energy required to actualize potential often lies invisible and dormant until it is aroused through the means described in this book. These means include connecting with others in ways that enrich and energize us, clarity of thought regarding our values and beliefs, commitment to a compelling purpose, the magnet-like force of richly detailed vision of that which we desire to create, and the motivation produced by an expanded set of possibilities. Human potential and energy become visible as they manifest themselves through our words and our actions and the world changes.

Two of the most significant barriers to the realization of human potential—resignation and dependency—are also often invisible to the casual observer. By recognizing and naming them, we begin the process of shifting from resignation to possibility and from dependency to a sense of personal power.

FOCUS ON LEADERS

This book focuses on the leader's role in actualizing human potential and unleashing individual and organizational energy. Leaders do so by connecting people to larger purposes and to one another and by culti-vating in their organizations transformational professional learning and breakthrough thinking. I focus on leaders—a category that in schools includes teacher leaders as well as principals and district administrators—because I believe that both formal and informal leaders have the capacity to make a tremendous difference in their organizations through their beliefs, values, intentions, and interactions.

A leader's work in actualizing human potential and unlocking energy is both personal and intensely interpersonal. It begins within each of us and radiates outward as we clarify our purposes, represent our views to others, improve the quality of our relationships, and shape the culture of our organizations. It is about individuals making a profound difference in the world around them, whether that world is their friends and families, their organizations, their communities, their nation, or the planet.

Because leaders' thoughts, emotions, and behaviors affect the moods and performance of countless others, this book views these qualities as critical but often neglected attributes of leadership. "Every one of our thoughts, emotions, and behaviors has an energy consequence, for better or for worse," Jim Loehr and Tony Schwarz (2003) point out in *The Power of Full Engagement*. "The ultimate measure of our lives is not how much time we spend on the planet, but rather how much energy we invest in the time we have" (p. 4).

Jane Dutton (2003) adds another dimension to this topic in *Energize Your Workplace*. "[L]eaders can make a profound difference in activating and renewing energy by building and sustaining high-quality connections . . . ," she writes. "High-quality connections contribute substantially to individuals' well-being and work performance. They also contribute significantly to an organization's capacity for collaboration, coordination, learning, and adaptation, as well as its ability to keep people committed and loyal" ("Executive Summary").

In *Shaking Up the School House* (2001), Phil Schlechty argues that it is imperative that school leaders be "transformational" rather than "transactional." "Transformational leadership," he writes, "requires the leader to embrace and cause others to embrace new and revolutionary assumptions" rather than " . . . only to improve operational effectiveness based on well-established and commonly accepted assumptions" (p. 164).

My dictionary defines "transform" as a "change in composition or structure" and says it "implies a major change in form, nature, or function." It defines "breakthrough" as "a sudden advance especially in knowledge or technique." David Perkins (2000) says "breakthrough thinking" is a "cognitive snap" and " . . . creativity that makes a decisive break with the past" (p. 6). It is my goal to assist the reader in generating breakthrough thinking that transforms relationships among everyone in schools and dramatically improves the quality of student and educator learning.

Breakthroughs and transformations occur in many ways. Sometimes urgency in the face of life and death problems creates breakthroughs, as has been the case in wartime when bold new procedures were tried in the field to save lives. Sometimes it is a powerful moment of individual epiphany and reevaluation such as that experienced by an attorney who says he was led to a career in the ministry after he sat in a beautiful natural setting listening to a performance of the World Youth Symphony Orchestra. At other times, it is a subtle or not-so-subtle shift in perspective that comes from the words of another, such as those reported by Marlo Thomas (2002) in *The Right Words at the Right Time*. For instance, she cites film director Mike Nichols's experience of breakthrough: "Two or three times in my life, I have read or heard something that seemed in a moment to change me so palpably that I actually heard or felt a click, a sound, tumblers falling into place. . . . [I]t is simply the experience of becoming somebody slightly different, somebody new, the next you" (p. 238).

More than ever, educational leaders live in a results-oriented world with unprecedented external expectations for high levels of student achievement on standardized tests. My aim in *Leading for Results* is not only to help you meet those expectations, but to assist you in creating the additional results you value in your school, school system, and life. Because I believe significant change in organizations begins with transformational change in their leaders—as Gandhi put it, "We must become the change we seek in the world"—this book will assist you in developing ways of thinking, speaking, and acting that are particularly powerful in achieving your goals.

While leadership that promotes continuous improvements in student and adult learning includes many attributes and qualities, I believe that the most important of these can be reduced to a set of beliefs and abilities that I term "results skills." They include:

- Clarity of thought regarding intentions and assumptions;
- Deep understanding of important subjects;
- The capacity to create;
- Empowering beliefs;
- The concise and consistent expression of those intentions and beliefs in the spirit of dialogue;
- Committed listening; and
- Continuous innovation in the methods used to achieve our goals.

I explore each of these results skills in the chapters that follow.

I recognize that the readers of this book are already likely to possess highly developed skills. You may have one or more college degrees and hold a responsible position within the education community and may serve on important committees. Because I start with the assumption that you are already successful, this book provides a series of invitations to try one or more of the ideas or skills presented here to determine if they will aid you in achieving that which is most important to you.

My Assumptions

The views I express in *Leading for Results* are grounded in the following assumptions:

> **Leaders matter. Therefore, significant changes in organizations begin with significant changes in what leaders think (depth of understanding and beliefs), say (the speech forms we use and the content of our speech), and do (a continuous flow of powerful actions within a culture of interpersonal accountability).**

The habits that produce significant advances in schooling—particularly improvements in teaching and learning—begin with significant change in leaders. That means leaders first consider how their own assumptions, understanding of significant issues, and behaviors may be preserving current practices. They then initiate a disciplined process of developing habits of mind and practice that will assist them in achieving their purposes.

> **Resignation and dependency on the part of principals and teachers are major barriers to quality teaching in all classrooms and the successful learning of all students.**

When spoken by teachers and principals, the phrases "There's nothing I can do" and "Tell me what to do" are two of the most damaging and disempowering unintended consequences of school reform efforts. The ideas and skills I present in this book are a means by which school leaders can move themselves and those with whom they interact to more empowered and enabling points of view.

> **High-quality professional interactions within a high-performance culture are a prerequisite to quality teaching in all classrooms.**

Most of the important forms of professional learning occur in daily interactions among teachers in which they work together to improve lessons, deepen one another's understanding of content, analyze student work, examine various data sources on student performance, and solve the myriad of problems they face each day. From this perspective, teacher-to-teacher communication about teaching and learning is the most powerful and sustained source of professional learning and instructional improvement. Consequently, one of the most important responsibilities of school leaders is the development of a high-performance culture that has at its heart mutual respect and trust, collaboration, and continuous improvement and in which generative human connections can thrive.

> **Because instructional and cultural change is intensely interpersonal, it is essential that leaders consistently apply communication and problem-solving skills that promote productive relationships founded on qualities such as clarity of values and purpose, candor, trust, and integrity.**

Deep and far-reaching improvements originate in relationships formed within strong, purpose-focused, and action-oriented communities. Improving instruction and building culture are relationship intensive and often conflict ridden. Unless leaders successfully address the complex and often emotionally laden interpersonal demands of school leadership, schools won't achieve long-term improvements in teaching and student achievement. That requires that principals and teachers take the lead in establishing a high-performance culture.

> **The intellectual and creative capacity of educators— particularly principals and teachers—to make significant improvements in teaching and learning is an underdeveloped and untapped resource.**

The most successful schools are "innovation machines" in which students and adults continually invent better ways of achieving their purposes and that amplify the best practices of teachers across the faculty. Teachers in such schools tap research and best practice, but they do so as peers and partners with researchers and policy makers who recognize and value their contributions and talents. Unless such appreciative and respectful relationships are in place, we cannot create schools in which all students and teachers learn and perform at high levels.

> **Sustained action-oriented professional learning by all principals and teachers is essential in creating schools with quality teaching in every classroom.**

High-quality professional development is intellectually rigorous, attends to both content knowledge and teaching methods, enhances the quality of professional judgment, and embeds teachers in a supportive community of professional practice. High-quality professional development enables teachers to bridge the "knowing-doing" gap that is prevalent in virtually all schools so that new practices are initiated and sustained in classrooms.

> **Planning and implementation decisions about professional learning matter—whether those decisions are made at the federal, district, state, or school levels. This means that district administrators, principals, and teachers must consistently advocate for the most powerful forms of professional learning.**

Visa founder Dee Hock provides a standard against which policy may be measured: "Have a simple, clear purpose," he says, "which gives rise to complex, intelligent behavior rather than complex rules and regulations that give rise to simplistic thinking and stupid behavior." Effective planning and policy decisions, therefore, provide a clear, compelling purpose grounded in improved practice and student learning; develops in teachers and administrators complex, intelligent behavior; and provides resources to maintain this effort over many years.

Planning and policy decisions made by school improvement committees, district staff development committees, and policy-making bodies can guide teachers and principals toward the most powerful forms of professional learning or lead them toward low-level learning and the dependency and resignation discussed above.

(I recommend that readers preview "How to Use This Book," before engaging in the following activities.)

Examine Your Assumptions

Write your assumptions regarding the significance of what leaders think, say, and do, stating them as succinctly and powerfully as possible. Make simple, declarative statements of your beliefs. For instance, you may believe "Leaders really don't matter because teachers are the ones who ultimately affect student learning." Share your assumptions with colleagues in the spirit of dialogue.

_____

_____

_____

_____

_____

_____

Deepen Your Understanding

Clarify in writing your views on the impact of leaders in achieving organizational goals and the qualities of leaders that produce that effect. Discuss your views with others.

Engage in Next Action Thinking

Specify actions you will take to apply what you have learned in this chapter about leadership and by what date you will take those actions.

_____

_____

_____

_____

_____

_____

REFERENCES

Dutton, J. (2003). *Energize your workplace.* San Francisco: Jossey-Bass.

Loehr, J., & Schwarz, T. (2003). *The power of full engagement.* New York: The Free Press.

Perkins, D. (2000). *The eureka effect: The art and logic of breakthrough thinking.* New York: W.W. Norton.

Ray, P., & Anderson, S. R. (2000). *The cultural creatives: How 50 million people are changing the world.* New York: Three Rivers Press.

Schlechty, P. (2001). *Shaking up the school house.* San Francisco: Jossey-Bass.

Thomas, M. (2002). *The right words at the right time.* New York: Atria Books.

How to
Use This Book

All acts of understanding require accessing prior knowledge and applying it to guide the noticing, framing, and connecting of new ideas and events to what is already encoded in memory. This is an active process, not a passive encoding of information.

—James Spillane, Brian Reiser, & Todd Reimer

Only when students can articulate in writing the basic principles they are learning . . . can we be sure that they are internalizing those principles in an intellectually coherent way.

—Richard Paul

My assumptions: The major purposes of professional learning are to deepen understanding, transform beliefs and assumptions, and create a stream of continuous actions that change habits and affect practice. Such learning most often occurs through sustained attention, study, and action.

I intend *Leading for Results: Transforming Teaching, Learning, and Relationships in Schools* to be a tool to inform your professional learning and guide your actions. From my perspective, the major purposes of professional learning are to deepen understanding, transform beliefs and assumptions, and create a stream of continuous actions that change habits and affect practice. To those ends, I bring you what I regard as leading-edge ideas and practices about improving the quality of leadership, teaching, and student learning and ask you to seriously consider their implications for your work through sustained attention, study, and action of the kind promoted in this book.

While there is no single correct way to use this book, I believe its value will best be realized when used by a study group whose members are committed to improving professional learning, teaching, and leadership in their school or school system. Chapters may be studied in any order or used in combination as starting points for dialogue, professional learning, and action related to the topic at hand.

In subsequent chapters, I will seldom include citations to the work of others because I intend this book to be an expression of my views based on my reading and experience in the field. I want you to interact with the ideas to develop your own views rather than simply surrender your point of view to "experts." Quotations are highlighted to stimulate your thinking and promote dialogue. Readers interested in a fuller exploration of most of the ideas presented here will be able to find countless columns, articles, and books that address them, including my earlier book, *Designing Powerful Professional Development for Teachers and Principals,* available at www.nsdc.org/library/leaders/sparksbook.cfm.

Some of my favorite nonfiction books use stories or anecdotes to illustrate important points. (Please see Chapter 9 to consider the value of stories in promoting improvement.) I have shied away from such examples here, however, because the appropriate use of the ideas and skills presented here are context bound. That makes it difficult to provide a succinct example to illustrate external variables and internal thought processes that affect a particular course of action. In addition, some of my most compelling illustrations come from real-life situations and would be virtually impossible to recount without compromising the anonymity of those involved. So, to the best of your ability, please reflect on your own personal and professional lives as a source of stories that illustrate and make personally meaningful the ideas I present.

ORGANIZATION OF THE BOOK

Leading for Results is divided into three sections:

"Transformation Through Clarity and Creation" addresses the power of clarity of thought, breakthrough thinking, and human creativity. These chapters describe ways to develop clarity regarding intentions, values, assumptions, and actions.

"Transformation Through Interpersonal Influence" provides insight into specific results-oriented ways of speaking, listening, and interacting. These chapters present ways to use these skills to achieve a school's most important purposes.

"Transformation Through Professional Learning and Doing" provides an overview of the attributes of the most effective forms of professional development for improving staff and student learning. These chapters consider how to develop new professional habits of thought and behavior and bridge the knowing-doing gap.

Each chapter promotes deeper understanding, transformational learning, and "next action thinking" as described below.

Deeper Understanding: Some forms of professional learning are shallow. Because of the design of the experience, participants' learning skims across the surface of complex topics. While superficial learning has its place in creating awareness of issues, it is far too often the sum and substance of professional development for teachers and administrators.

A common example is teachers who attend an introductory workshop on cooperative learning and leave knowing only that the process involves students working together in small groups. Likewise, principals may superficially learn the procedures of "walk-throughs" as an instructional leadership activity but not truly understand the subtleties of what they might observe nor how to discuss their observations with teachers.

Therefore, each chapter asks you to elaborate your learning in various ways to deepen your understanding and to create meaning and a context for the learning. Deep understanding typically requires sustained thought and engagement with a subject. Such engagement asks learners of all ages to paraphrase what they are learning, draw inferences from it, and connect new learning to prior knowledge and experience. It also asks them to synthesize and evaluate what they are learning; to write, speak, prepare mind maps and other graphic organizers; to engage in dialogue; and to develop action plans for applying their learning.

Transformational Learning: Because beliefs and assumptions (what we hold to be true about a subject) exert a powerful force on our behavior and professional practice, it is critically important that leaders examine their own beliefs to determine if they are furthering their purposes or impeding them. Transformational learning at the level of beliefs and assumptions can occur through many means, but two of the most common are dialogue and engagement in activities that evoke strong emotions and/or create cognitive dissonance. In dialogue, participants surface and explore their assumptions in a nonthreatening setting and gradually open themselves to seeing the world from the perspective of others. Strong emotion and cognitive dissonance may be evoked when leaders make site visits, shadow or interview students, or are confronted by disaggregated data that break through walls of denial.

For the purposes of this book, I encourage you to use dialogue whenever possible to deepen your understanding of the topic and to promote transformational learning. To stimulate this form of interaction, I include my own assumptions in each chapter whenever appropriate. In the spirit of dialogue, I invite you to identify and express your own assumptions on those topics and to encourage others with whom you interact to do the same. To stimulate and clarify your thinking and to provide balance, I will provide in the "Examine Your Assumptions" section of each chapter beliefs that I have heard expressed by educators that are contrary to my own.

"Dialogue . . . imposes a rigorous discipline on the participants," Daniel Yankelovich (1999) writes in *The Magic of Dialogue: Transforming Conflict Into Cooperation.* "[W]hen dialogue is done skillfully, the results can be extraordinary: long-standing stereotypes dissolved, mistrust overcome, mutual understanding achieved, visions shaped and grounded in shared purpose, people previously at odds with one another aligned on objectives and strategies, new common ground discovered, new perspectives and insights gained, new levels of creativity stimulated, and bonds of community strengthened" (p. 16).

The discipline that Yankelovich recommends (and that I suggest you use in discussing this and other chapters) includes equality among participants, an absence of coercive influences, listening with empathy, and bringing assumptions into the open while suspending judgment. Those seeking to maximize the benefits they receive from this book may wish to read *The Magic of Dialogue* or *Dialogue: Rediscovering the Transforming Power of Conversation* by Linda Ellinor and Glenna Gerard (1998).

"Next Action Thinking:" A stream of continuous actions is required to change habits to improve leadership and instructional practices. Deep understanding and clarity regarding assumptions are of limited value unless they are followed by commitments to such actions and a sense of interpersonal accountability for completing them.

In *Getting Things Done: The Art of Stress-Free Productivity* (2001), David Allen writes, "Over the years, I have noticed an extraordinary shift in energy and productivity whenever individuals and groups installed 'What's the next action?' as a fundamental and consistently asked question" (p. 236). The result, he says, would be that " . . . no meeting or discussion will end, and no interaction cease, without a clear determination of whether or not some action is needed—and if it is, what it will be, or at least who has responsibility for it" (p. 236). Allen argues that " . . . shifting your focus to something that your mind perceives as a doable, completable task will create a real increase in positive energy, direction, and motivation" (p. 242).

My goal is that you use this book to deepen your understanding of its topics, shift your beliefs to empower yourself and others, and set in motion a stream of powerful goal-focused actions within a system of interpersonal accountability that includes regular reflection on the impact of those actions. To aid you in implementing the ideas and skills in this book, I offer its content in bite-size chapters that can be digested over a period of weeks or months.

Simply reading these entries, however, is unlikely to improve your understanding or use of these ideas. I encourage you to slow down to ponder the meaning and implications of what you are reading so you can intellectually interact with the ideas. Write about and teach others what you are learning. Creatively combine these ideas for your unique purposes. What is ultimately important is the quality of discussion and intensity of motivation provided by a study group, your depth of engagement with the ideas, and the actions you take as a consequence of that understanding.

EXAMINE YOUR ASSUMPTIONS

Write your assumptions regarding the significance of what leaders think, say, and do, stating them as succinctly and powerfully as possible. Make simple, declarative statements of your beliefs. For instance, you may believe "The major reason for professional development is to meet district, state, and federal requires. It doesn't serve any other purposes." Share your assumptions with colleagues in the spirit of dialogue.

_____

_____

_____

_____

_____

Deepen Your Understanding

Describe in writing and discuss with others the methods you use when you want to understand a subject more deeply. Consider which of them might be most effective in promoting your learning from this book.

_____

_____

_____

_____

_____

_____

Engage in Next Action Thinking

Specify actions you will take to apply those learning methods as you study this book.

_____

_____

_____

_____

_____

_____

_____

REFERENCES

Allen, D. (2001). *Getting things done: The art of stress-free productivity.* New York: Viking.

Ellinor, L., & Gerard, G. (1998). *Dialogue: Rediscovering the transforming power of conversation.* New York: John Wiley & Sons.

Yankelovich, D. (1999). *The magic of dialogue: Transforming conflict into cooperation.* New York: Simon & Schuster.

Acknowledgments

I am immensely grateful to Dave Ellis and Bill Rentz, president and vice president, respectively, of the Brande Foundation, for stimulating many of the ideas in this book. Through the foundation, Dave gave me the deeply appreciated gift of life coaching and demonstrated in his own writing and speaking the power of clarity of thought and of simply expressed ideas. Bill Rentz served ably as my life coach and partner in the development of a "results skills" curriculum out of which a section of this book grew. Dave and Bill's deep belief in the capacity of individuals and groups to create the life of their dreams in all aspects of their lives has informed and inspired my work.

I want to thank the National Staff Development Council (NSDC) trustees, past and present, who have encouraged me and other council staff members to extend our thinking into new areas and to disseminate our ideas widely. I have been truly honored to work with these individuals and to benefit from their leadership regarding NSDC's ambitious goals for professional learning in schools.

I owe a huge debt of gratitude to the core professional staff of the National Staff Development Council—Stephanie Hirsh, Joan Richardson, Joellen Killion, and Leslie Miller—whose incredible competence and ability to work both independently and as part of various teams make it possible for me to have the intellectual space necessary to prepare a book such as this one. In particular, I want to thank Joan Richardson, NSDC's director of publications, whose careful and thoughtful editing of this manuscript and coordination of this project with Corwin Press have made significant contributions to the quality of this book.

In addition, I would like to extend my appreciation to Rachel Livsey of Corwin Press and Sanford Robinson of Sage Publications for their valuable contribution to this effort. While the author's name appears on book covers, the individuals who work invisibly behind the scenes have a large effect on the quality of to develop the book you hold in your hands.

Whatever value this book holds for its readers is due in large part to the thousands of educators with whom I have interacted over the years. Their perspectives and experiences have shaped my views and kept me grounded in the day-to-day lives of teachers and school leaders whose work gives purpose to my writing.

About the Author

 **Dennis Sparks** has been executive director of the 10,000-member National Staff Development Council since 1984. Before this position, he was an independent educational consultant and director of the Northwest Staff Development Center, a state and federally funded teacher center in Livonia, Michigan.

Dr. Sparks has also been a teacher, counselor, and codirector of an alternative high school. He completed his Ph.D. in counseling at the University of Michigan in 1976 and has taught at several universities. He speaks frequently throughout North America on topics such as powerful staff development and effective teaching.

He is author of *Designing Powerful Professional Development for Teachers and Principals* (NSDC, 2002); *Conversations that Matter* (NSDC, 2001), a collection of his *JSD* interviews since 1991; coauthor with Stephanie Hirsh, *Learning to Lead, Leading to Learn* (NSDC, 2000); coauthor with Joan Richardson, *What Is Staff Development Anyway?* (NSDC, 1998); and coauthor with Stephanie Hirsh, *A New Vision for Staff Development* (ASCD/NSDC, 1997).

Dr. Sparks's column appears each month in the newsletter, *Results*, a publication of the National Staff Development Council. His interviews with leading educational thinkers appear in *JSD*, a quarterly magazine published by the council. In addition, his articles have appeared in a variety of publications, including *Educational Leadership*, *Phi Delta Kappan*, *The American School Board Journal*, *The Principal*, and *The School Administrator*.

All of Dr. Sparks's interviews and articles are accessible on the NSDC Web site at www.nsdc.org/library/authors/sparks.cfm.

PART I

Transformation Through Clarity and Creation

Long-distance winners often have disarmingly simple mission statements. When the question was put to Jonas Salk, he replied: "To reduce human suffering."

—John R. O'Neil

People with clear minds are like magnets.

—Wilma Mankiller

The chapters in Part I: Transformation Through Clarity and Creation are based on a few simple premises:

- We affect the world through clarity regarding our most fundamental values and purposes.
- Intentions aligned with our individual and collective values and purposes are particularly powerful in producing the results we most desire.
- Having multiple, well-considered pathways to achieving large, important goals significantly increases the likelihood of producing those results.
- Educators' capacity to invent solutions to educational problems is a powerful, untapped resource for improvement.

Because school leaders' most important responsibilities are helping schools set inspiring goals and engaging staff members in creating the means to achieve them, leaders' intentions and the way they are expressed have a profound effect on the organizations they lead. Consequently, one of the most important skills possessed by leaders is clarity of thought and speech about what they believe and want to create. And because the clarity and the sense of empowerment leaders provide are contagious, individuals and organizations are transformed when these qualities are brought with persistence to various settings.

Here is a famous example of the power of the succinct expression of intention aligned with a fundamental purpose: In 1940, Winston Churchill spoke to the British House of Commons. In his first speech as Prime Minister, he said: "I would say to the House, as I said to those who have joined this government: 'I have nothing to offer but blood, toil, tears and sweat.' . . . You ask, what is our policy? I can say: It is to wage war, by sea, land, and air, with all our might and with all the strength that God can give us. . . . You ask, what is our aim? I can answer in one word: It is victory, victory at all costs, victory in spite of all terror, victory, however long and hard the road may be; for without victory, there is no survival."

While we all do not possess the oratorical skills of Winston Churchill nor do we lead in lofty matters of state, Churchill's passionate commitment to his purpose and the clarity of his aim are qualities each of us can adapt to our own settings. And when leaders assist teachers in connecting with deeper purposes and tapping into their own creative powers, the passion and commitment that are generated will fuel sustained professional learning and continuous improvement in teaching and learning.

CHAPTER 1

Clarify Your Fundamental Choices, Values, and Purposes

When people make a fundamental choice to be true to what is highest in them, or when they make a choice to fulfill a purpose in their life, they can easily accomplish many changes that seemed impossible or improbable in the past.

—Robert Fritz

One fundamental choice is the primary influence on all other choices; every day you can choose consciously to move consistently, persistently, and boldly in the direction of your dreams.

—David McNally & Karl Speak

My assumptions: We shape our future and the future of the organizations we serve through the fundamental choices we make and the values and purposes we select. Clearly defined fundamental choices, values, and purposes organize our activities, keep us on track, and sustain our efforts. They also are filters through which we can consider the desirability of our intentions and beliefs.

F ew individuals become teachers who do not possess a healthy dose of idealism about making the world a better place through education. And teachers who become administrators often do so because they want to have an even larger effect on the lives of young people. Over time, however, educators may have lost touch with the passion their values and purposes initially infused into their professional lives, or their experiences have led them to doubt the possibility of achieving such lofty purposes.

Clarity regarding our values and purpose is an important means of reclaiming a sense of direction, power, and energy. Creating a succinct statement of your life purpose and a list of values requires a period of reflection, but it can usually be done in an hour or less with periodic updating and will serve as a reference point for all your activities. In addition, the ability to succinctly express our values and purposes in conversations often empowers others to do

> New patterns of behavior usually only occur when I, the change agent, have a new viewpoint and a new purpose.
>
> —Robert Quinn

the same. Such honest exchange of views can have a significant effect on a school's culture and the learning and performance of staff members and students.

Like professional purposes and values, "fundamental choices" guide our actions. They express our deepest aspirations, possess a tremendous power to shape and sustain high performance, provide a filter for planning one's activities, and sustain motivation during difficult times.

"A fundamental choice," Robert Fritz (1989) writes, "is a choice in which you commit yourself to a basic life orientation or a basic state of being" (p. 188). Examples include being the predominant creative force in your life, being true to what is highest within you, and being healthy and free. Primary choices, Fritz says, are those we make about the major results we wish to create, and secondary choices are the steps we take

> If you want to build a ship, don't gather your people and ask them to provide wood, prepare tools, assign tasks. Call them together and raise in their minds the longing for the endless sea.
>
> —Antoine de Saint-Exupery

toward achieving those results. Primary choices are often called results, goals, or objectives; secondary choices are strategies or action plans.

Fundamental choices, Fritz says (1989), provide the foundation for primary and secondary choices. "When people make a fundamental choice to be true to what is highest in them, or when they make a choice to fulfill a purpose in their life, they can easily accomplish many changes that seemed impossible or improbable in the past" (p. 189).

> We make the most lasting and vivid impression when people witness us being true to our beliefs, staying in alignment with who and what we really are.
>
> —David McNally & Karl Speak

On the other hand, school leaders sometimes make fundamental, primary, and secondary choices that fuel "slow death spirals." For instance, principals may decide, consciously or unconsciously, that, no matter what, they will avoid conflicts with their supervisors or teachers. Because well-managed conflicts are important in decision making related to complex, important issues about which educators hold strong opinions, such disagreements are unlikely to be aired and resolved when leaders avoid such conflict.

> To be fully engaged, we must be physically energized, emotionally connected, mentally focused and spiritually aligned with a purpose beyond our immediate self-interest.
>
> —Jim Loehr & Tony Schwartz

Educational leaders sometimes can also make fundamental choices that lead to deep changes in themselves and the organizations in which they work, which lead to significant improvements in student learning. A superintendent, for example, who has made a strong, public commitment to all students having a competent, caring teacher will approach all relevant decisions with a frame of reference formed by that commitment.

> How different our lives are when we really know what is deeply important to us, and, keeping that picture in mind, we manage ourselves each day to be and do what really matters.
>
> —Stephen Covey

The power of fundamental choices can be harnessed to motivate and sustain change. Robert Quinn (2000) describes the power of fundamental choices this way: "The individuals, groups, teams, and organizations will not change until they can identify and embrace their potential, that is, really grasp what they are capable of achieving. This will not happen until one person, somewhere, makes a fundamental choice and begins to demonstrate a new way of being. This will result in new actions, words, and commitment" (p. 94).

This occurs, Quinn (2000) contends, because our enthusiasm and commitment are contagious. "People around us are moved in ways that are subtle but powerful. We become living symbols of a new vision. We send out new signals to everyone around us, and if we are in an organization, our very presence disrupts old routines.... A new dialogue is born and the culture in which we are participating begins to change" (p. 113).

> We recognize that the world changes only when individuals shift to living with a new set of values, beliefs, attitudes, and assumptions.
>
> —George Land & Beth Jarman

EXAMINE YOUR ASSUMPTIONS

Write your assumptions regarding the importance of clarifying your purposes, values, and fundamental choices, stating them as succinctly and powerfully as possible. For instance, you may believe that "People have so little say over their actions that it's a waste of time trying to figure out our purposes and values." Share your assumptions with colleagues in the spirit of dialogue.

_____

_____

_____

_____

_____

_____

DEEPEN YOUR UNDERSTANDING

Define in writing the fundamental choices you want to guide your life (for instance, living each day as a creative act). In addition, write a succinct statement of your life's purpose. Begin with the phrase "My life's purpose is to. . . ." Do the same with your professional purpose. List several of your most important professional values. Make a second list of your life values if they are different. Share your

statements and lists with others and be prepared to revise what you
have written based on the discussion.

_____

_____

_____

_____

_____

_____

ENGAGE IN NEXT ACTION THINKING

Specify actions you will take based on your fundamental choices,
values, or purposes, and by what date you will take those actions.

_____

_____

_____

_____

_____

_____

REFERENCES

Fritz, R. (1989). *The path of least resistance.* New York: Fawcett Columbine.
Quinn, R. (2000). *Change the world: How ordinary people can accomplish extraordinary results.* San Francisco: Jossey-Bass.

CHAPTER 2

Clarify Your Intentions

You will bring into your life whatever it is that you have the most clarity about. The trouble is, most people have a great deal of clarity about what it is they don't want.

—Susan Scott

Man's vitality is as great as his intentionality: they are interdependent.

—Paul Tillich

> **My assumptions: Clearly formulated and expressed intentions and pride about what we want are powerful tools in creating the results we desire. Almost always, our desires are trusted guides for the future of our organizations.**

Knowing what we want and being proud of it increases the likelihood we will achieve the results we seek. Intentions described in rich detail offer direction for their achievement and make it more likely we will recognize valuable opportunities.

Telling the truth about what we want in our lives is essential to being effective leaders and human beings in relationship to one another. Naming and describing our desires and generating multiple pathways to realizing them (about which more will be said in Chapter 7) empowers us. Our empowerment, in turn, empowers those with whom we interact.

A method I use to identify and clarify my intentions is to write them on three-by-five-inch index cards, one per card. A computer might be used for the same purpose. I begin with the sentence stem, "I want . . . ," and write whatever comes to mind. At the end of a 15-minute session, I may have 20 to 25 intentions, some of which

I will simply throw away upon second thought. I might use such a session for the broad purpose of gathering intentions related to all subjects that come to mind or in a more focused way related to a particular problem or issue. I use the back of index cards to add descriptive detail regarding the intention and possible action steps.

> No wind favors him who has no destined port.
>
> —Montaigne

I encourage you to capture in writing your intention, specific details or images of attaining that goal, and the steps you will take to reach it. Writing can crystallize and freeze our thinking so we can examine and strengthen it. I recommend writing a brief essay or constructing a mind map about what achieving the goal would look and feel like and the effects it will have on people who encounter it.

Our complaints (and those of others) are another means of better understanding our intentions and commitments. One way of addressing the dispiriting effects of complaints, particularly about professional issues, is to recognize that behind most complaints lies a commitment to something of value to the individual. Thwarting that commitment activates the complaint. Allowing individuals and groups to identify and express these intentions and commitments and to consider ways of realizing them is a powerful tool for achieving results.

> Dare to be remarkable.
>
> —Jane Gentry

Robert Kegan and Lisa Lahey (2001) describe this phenomenon in *How the Way We Talk Can Change the Way We Work.* "[F]or every commitment we genuinely hold to bring about some important change, there is another commitment we hold that has the effect of preventing the change," they write (p. 63). For instance, a principal who is committed to ensuring quality teaching for all students may find that she also has a not entirely conscious countervailing commitment to avoiding conflict with staff members.

> You maximize the likelihood of developing creative and innovative solutions by setting aside presumed human, physical, information, and financial constraints that limit your vision.
>
> —Gerald Nadler & Shozo Hibino

Kegan and Lahey also contend that "Big Assumptions" firmly hold these countervailing commitments in place. They say individuals treat these assumptions as accurate representations of reality and believe dire consequences will follow if they are violated. Big Assumptions derive their influence because they typically pass under the radar of our conscious awareness and because they presume dire consequences. For instance, in the example above, the principal may believe conflict will quickly escalate out of control and result in anger, hurt feelings, or even irreparably damaged relationships.

Kegan and Lahey recommend that individuals and groups:

- Explore their countervailing commitments (I'm committed to quality teaching for all students in this school, but I'm also committed to minimizing conflict and getting along with everyone);
- Examine the "Big Assumptions" that anchor the competing commitment (If I truthfully say my views, it will provoke conflict and the consequences will be horrible); and
- Design simple, low-risk experiments to determine the validity of their assumptions (At a grade-level meeting, explaining her views on ways to strengthen teaching).

EXAMINE YOUR ASSUMPTIONS

Write your assumptions regarding the value of clarifying what you want, stating them as succinctly and powerfully as possible. For instance, you may believe "My job as a leader is to serve other people so that they get what they want. My desires are secondary to their purposes." Share your assumptions with colleagues in the spirit of dialogue.

_____

_____

_____

_____

_____

_____

DEEPEN YOUR UNDERSTANDING

Teach one or more people about the value of clarifying our professional and personal intentions.

For example, the next time you make plans for a meeting, say out loud to the participants that your intention is to arrive five minutes before the meeting is scheduled to start to ensure that you are prepared to begin the meeting at the announced time.

> Many of us hold ourselves back from imaging a desired outcome unless someone can show us how to get there. Unfortunately, that's backwards in terms of how our minds work to generate and recognize solutions and methods.
>
> —David Allen

ENGAGE IN NEXT ACTION THINKING

List at least 10 things you want at work. List everything that comes to mind. Make a second list of things you want in your personal life. Add details to improve the clarity of your intentions. Review your list each day, adding, deleting, or revising items as appropriate. Set a goal to have at least 50 items on each list within a month.

_____

_____

_____

_____

_____

_____

_____

REFERENCE

Kegan, R., & Lahey, L. (2001). *How the way we talk can change the way we work.* San Francisco: Jossey-Bass.

CHAPTER 3

Establish Stretch Goals

Make no little plans; they have no magic to stir men's blood and probably in themselves will not be realized. Make big plans; aim high in hope and work remembering that a noble, logical diagram once recorded will never die.

—Daniel Hudson Burnham

If you limit your choices to what seems possible or reasonable, you disconnect yourself from what you truly want, and what is left is a compromise.

—Robert Fritz

> **My assumption: Ambitious goals are more likely to produce the deep changes in beliefs and practices that are essential in improving the learning of all students and in sustaining those changes over time.**

One theory of goal setting recommends setting modest, incremental goals because people are more likely to achieve them and to experience the motivation provided by that success. This motivation, in turn, leads to continued improvement.

Another theory says "stretch goals"—goals so large they seem impossible to achieve—and the deep changes they require for their attainment are more valuable in producing significant, lasting improvements in schools. The benefits of both processes can be obtained, however, when their strengths are blended. Stretch goals can stimulate deep change, while incremental "milestone" goals can provide mid-course markers of improvement (which could be viewed as incremental goals) and offer opportunities to celebrate success and experience the motivation provided by achieving them.

> [Big Hairy Audacious Goals] . . . may be daunting and perhaps risky, but the adventure, excitement, and challenge of it grabs people in the gut, gets their juices flowing, and creates immense forward momentum.
>
> —James Collins & Jerry Porras

Stretch goals are important because most individuals and organizations underestimate their ability to improve. For instance, teachers or administrators may believe students from particular families or ethnic and racial groups are less capable of certain types of learning. That's why leaders in this field like Dave Ellis ask educators to set goals for "paradise" and then to reset them for "paradise times four" and David Allen encourages us to envision "wild success."

> Part of an organization's vision can be an ideal toward which we always strive without ever reaching it. Part of a vision must be attainable, lest the group lose hope.
>
> —Max DePree

Stretch goals by their very nature require important, deep changes in the organization. Achieving stretch goals (some individuals use the term "BHAG" to prompt themselves to establish *Big, Hairy, Audacious Goals*) requires unrelenting focus, clarity of thought, consistent communication, alignment of resources, innovation, discipline, and teamwork. For example, the goal that all students will read at grade level or higher when they leave this school is likely to require significant alterations in curriculum, assessment, teaching methods, leadership practices, after-school programs, and engagement with parents.

> Leaders who get the best results combine an ability to set inspiring goals and a willingness to admit that they don't know exactly how to accomplish those goals.
>
> —Kate Sweetman

Examine Your Assumptions

> [C]onstriction of the possible could be the single largest obstacle in the way of renewal.
>
> —John O'Neil

> In striving to attain big things, the little things become easy, but in striving to attain only little things, even they become hard.
>
> —C. T. Gilbreath

Write your assumptions regarding the value of stretch goals in stimulating significant improvement, stating them as succinctly and powerfully as possible. For instance, you may believe "Stretch goals by their very nature set up teachers for dispiriting frustration and failure, feelings that are a major barrier to continuous improvement." Share your assumptions with colleagues in the spirit of dialogue.

_____

_____

_____

_____

_____

_____

_____

Deepen Your Understanding

> When we have successfully experienced a deep change, it inspires us to encourage others to undergo a similar experience. We are all potential change agents. As we discipline our talents, we deepen our perceptions about what is possible.
>
> —Robert Quinn

Stretch your intentions by detailing the qualities and characteristics of the school you would create if you knew you could not fail in its implementation. As you conceptualize this school, plan it without knowing whether you would be a student, teacher, or principal and that you would play this role forever. Consider how your description might inform your current school improvement efforts.

_____

_____

_____

_____

_____

_____

_____

ENGAGE IN NEXT ACTION THINKING

Establish one or more stretch goals for your work or for your school, specifying actions you will take and by what date you will take those actions.

_____

_____

_____

_____

_____

_____

_____

CHAPTER 4

Create Successful Schools

The human capacity to invent and create is universal. . . . Perhaps the most powerful example in my own work is how relatively easy it is to create successful organizational change if you start with the assumption that people, like all life, are creative and good at change.

—Margaret Wheatley

If you want to predict the future, create it! This is precisely what school people now have the opportunity—and the imperative—to do.

—Roland Barth

> **My assumptions: Engagement in creative work energizes and increases teachers' and administrators' commitment to continuous improvement. Educators' capacity to invent solutions to educational problems is a powerful, untapped resource for improvement.**

Educators do not typically think of themselves as creators or inventors of school reform. Creativity is usually associated with designing interesting lessons or classroom projects, not schoolwide improvement strategies. Consequently, the design of more effective schools is usually left to "experts" who determine better ways of teaching or organizing schools or to policy makers who use legislation to increase the use of "best practices."

Almost all schools can make significant improvements in teaching and learning, I believe, by more effectively sharing the effective practices that are already being used within them and by inventing additional ways to promote student learning that are unique to that school. (More will be said about this in Chapter 22). After all, more often than not, the practices that reformers wish to spread among schools were initially invented by teachers and administrators who were creating innovative solutions to complex and important problems. In these schools, teachers' existing skills and creative capacity contributed to development of new practices and improved student learning.

> Inventing in the creative process is developing an original path between current reality and your vision. Convention is adopting a path others have already used and institutionalized. In school, we are usually taught the value of convention over invention.
>
> —Robert Fritz

At the same time, I want to underscore my belief that almost all schools can benefit from interacting with practitioners from other schools and from researchers or other sources of outside knowledge and skills. When teachers and principals initiate changes that encourage sharing effective practices and demonstrate their appreciation of the talents in their schools, teachers are more likely to reach out to other educators and to professional literature for energy and guidance.

> There's power in detail. When your destination is clear, you're more likely to arrive there. When your goals are loaded with specifics, you're more likely to know when you've met them.
>
> —Dave Ellis

My views about creativity have been heavily influenced by Robert Fritz (1989), whose ideas can be found in *The Path of Least Resistance.* Fritz believes the "structural tension" produced by the disparity between desired results and current reality precedes organizational creativity. Leaders can increase structural tension by developing a richly detailed vision of the desired results (for instance, being able to picture it as if it were

> In order most productively to access the conscious and unconscious resource available to you, you must have a clear picture in your mind of what success would look like, sound, and feel like. . . . When you focus on something . . . that focus instantly creates ideas and thought patterns you wouldn't have had otherwise.
>
> —David Allen

being enacted in a movie or described in a press release) and by grounding discussions of current reality in data and other forms of evidence.

> Our greatest joy no matter what our role comes from creating. In that process people become aware that they are able to do things they once thought were impossible. They have empowered themselves, which in turn empowers those with whom they interact.
>
> —Robert Quinn

Organizations, Fritz says, resolve this tension and move forward when they act to close the gap. Fritz recommends action plans that are simple to describe and to follow. Schools then use data to assess progress (the new current reality) and design new action plans. Each creative act and the success it generates produce professional learning and energy, which breeds more creativity, learning, energy, and success.

> Life is never more rich, more full, or more rewarding than when you are moving faithfully and persistently toward a compelling vision. When you are purposefully creating, you become fully alive.
>
> —David McNally & Karl Speak

Educators diminish organizational creativity when they have low expectations for students or themselves. It is also diminished when educators distort current reality through denial and minimizing and when they select strategies based on wishful thinking rather than a rigorous assessment of the strategies' ability to produce the desired result. All three problems find their way into school improvement planning:

> To artists, limitations are not liabilities, they are opportunities to find fresh, inventive solutions, to clarify key questions, to prioritize and to go deeper. . . . Creativity is sparked by boundaries.
>
> —Eric Booth

schools select modest outcomes because the faculty does not believe it can achieve more ambitious goals, planners define current reality through opinions and anecdotes rather than rigorous analysis of data, and schools select improvement strategies without thorough, tough-minded discussions about how to produce the intended outcome.

Creativity of the type described here involves far more than teachers and administrators spending an hour or two writing a vision statement and brainstorming strategies. Creating schools that have at their core high levels of student and adult learning and meaningful connections among members of the school community requires the

continuous development and use of professional knowledge and judgment. It also requires sustained study of professional literature, dialogue, and debate based on a candid exchange of views regarding vision, current reality, and strategies. The best

> The act of creating can bring out the best in people, because it is the natural motivator. No pep talk in the world, no matter how inspired, can touch the power of the involvement that creating generates.
>
> —Robert Fritz

way to develop these skills is by using them and by reflecting on the results. Sometimes that reflection may include soliciting feedback from skillful individuals outside the school who can provide an unbiased and useful perspective. No matter what approaches are used, skillful leadership by principals and teachers is essential if schools are to tap the creativity potential that resides within them.

EXAMINE YOUR ASSUMPTIONS

Write your assumptions regarding the role of creativity in designing schoolwide improvement efforts, stating them as succinctly and powerfully as possible. For instance, you may believe "Teachers do not have the knowledge, skill, nor interest to design effective improvement efforts, and even if they did, there is no reason to reinvent the wheel when a school can simply replicate what others have done." Share your assumptions with colleagues in the spirit of dialogue.

_____

_____

_____

_____

_____

_____

_____

DEEPEN YOUR UNDERSTANDING

Describe a time when you participated with others in creating a valued outcome and how it was the same or different from the approach recommended by Robert Fritz. For example, you might recall the process you followed in developing a new lesson, course, program, or initiative in your school or district. Discuss the success of your creative endeavor and how you felt during and after the process.

_____

_____

_____

_____

_____

_____

_____

_____

ENGAGE IN NEXT ACTION THINKING

Practice using structural tension to produce a result you desire in your work. It may be helpful to choose a short-term goal that can be achieved in a few days. Describe in detail both the desired results and current reality. Specify actions you will take to decrease the gap between your vision and current reality and by when you will take those actions.

_____

_____

_____

_____

_____

_____

_____

_____

REFERENCE

Fritz, R. (1989). *The path of least resistance.* New York: Fawcett Columbine.

CHAPTER 5

Identify Multiple Ways to Achieve Your Goals

The problem with trying to figure out how to achieve a goal before becoming committed to it is that the most effective means to a goal usually are invented in the process of achieving the goal itself.

—Dave Ellis

Most situations in life don't have a single right answer. . . . In my experience, the most effective actions arise when we live the question, 'What do we want to create?' . . . The key to all this is really pretty simple—believing that every person has the capacity to create.

—Peter Senge

> **My assumptions: Most goals can be achieved in many ways. This awareness frees us from "one-right-way" thinking and a dependence on "experts" to "advise" us. It also engages our creative capacities and promotes responsibility for selecting the most powerful strategies.**

For some people, realizing that most goals can be reached in many ways is a breakthrough thought. Thinking that there is a single right answer to complex educational problems and that "science" or an "expert" knows it—even though researchers and other experts often disagree—diminishes educators' belief in their capacity to innovate and their sense of responsibility for producing results. Dependency and resignation can easily become by-products of such thinking.

While educators' dependence on expert advice is often debilitating, reasoned opinion and the research and professional literature upon which it is based have their place in decision making. They can inform our assumptions, provide the substance for brainstorming during planning, and help us assess improvement strategies to determine their power and likelihood for achieving the desired result.

Getting a good idea begins with getting your hands on many ideas, Jonas Salk is credited with observing. Sometimes these ideas originate in our prior knowledge or experience. At other times, we may glean ideas from the professional literature, from consultants or other experts, or have conversations with those who have gone down this road before us. Our goal during this phase is not to find the "right" solution, but to expand the options for consideration. Some authorities on the creative process call this phase "saturation" as we fill our minds with information methodically sought from numerous sources.

> Stimulate your creativity by allowing for several alternative solutions and keeping them viable for as long as possible.
>
> —Gerald Nadler & Shozo Hibino

A common problem at this stage is for individual or groups to settle too quickly on the first strategy that comes to mind rather than seriously weighing the pros and cons of various approaches. Groups enter the "zone of wishful thinking" when they select a course of action without first determining its effectiveness. Another common problem in strategy selection is "group think," which occurs when individuals accede to the views of the group even though they doubt the wisdom of the decision.

Individuals and school groups can use a number of processes to improve the quality of the strategies they select. The first is to expand group thinking by brainstorming ways to achieve the goal. This process can sometimes be aided by reviewing research and other professional literature. Brainstorming is most effective, of course, when far-out, creative ideas are encouraged and participants feel emotionally safe to contribute to the process. Some facilitators prefer asking participants to create their own lists of ideas before the group begins brainstorming. Brainstorming honors the expertise that exists within the person or group, recognizes that most problems have more than one possible solution, and prevents us from prematurely selecting the first solution that comes to mind.

Sometimes a quick review of a brainstormed list reveals items for immediate action. At other times, it is critical to stand back from the list to determine the most powerful strategies, particularly when money and time for strategy implementation are in short supply. One way to do this is to apply the "The 80/20 Principle," which holds that

80% of the benefits will be found among 20% of the items on the list. A thoughtful discussion about which 20% of the items would produce 80% of the benefits may provide guidance about where to begin. In some situations, it may be helpful to further refine the strategies by using each item on the "20%" list as a source for further brainstorming. The "80/20 Principle" could again be applied to each list to identify the items likely to produce the maximum benefit.

Another means of vetting the original brainstormed list is to create a filter, such as a rubric or decision matrix, through which items must pass before being implemented. Research and other perspectives gained from professional literature may provide a basis for the filter. Other considerations may be included as well, such as expense and professional judgment regarding the strategy's impact. A simple process for doing this is asking individuals to indicate with a vote of one to five fingers their views on how successful the strategy or combination of strategies will be in achieving the intended result.

> The most interesting thing I've noticed is that there's a consistent order to the quality of ideas. You'd think the sixtieth idea would be the most lame, but for my purposes, which are to trigger leaps of imagination, it's often opposite. . . . The closer they get to the sixtieth idea, the more imaginative they become—because they have been forced to stretch their thinking.
>
> —Twyla Tharp

A way to double-check the power of the selected strategies is to articulate a "theory of change" that explains to someone outside the group its assumptions about how the proposed actions will accomplish their purposes. The process of making explicit these assumptions often reveals significant gaps in the plan that, if left unattended, would lead to failure. I have more to say on this topic in Chapter 9.

Discussions at this level of specificity often reveal the depth of the group's commitment to doing whatever is necessary to achieve the goal. Participants will sometimes report at this point that they thought the goal-setting and strategy development process was just another exercise to fulfill a bureaucratic requirement that no one had taken very seriously.

> [A] key characteristic distinguishing high-performing teams from lesser-performing ones is the ability to generate more options. This requires time for expansive thinking and idea generation from narrowing options through analysis and evaluation.
>
> —M. Kathryn Clubb

Individuals or groups typically find it useful to establish benchmarks to help measure progress and to help them know early on whether strategies are beginning to have their desired effect. These benchmarks also are a reminder to regularly celebrate progress.

Candor is particularly important during this process, particularly when the efficacy of various approaches is being weighed and strategies selected. Group members often have views about a strategy that are unexpressed because of the power of group opinion, the desire to minimize conflict with colleagues, or a lack of psychological safety and trust in the group. Waiting for the optimal conditions before speaking our truth may mean less effective ideas will be accepted, squandering precious resources and the goodwill of those affected by the decision. Chapter 9 addresses this subject.

Examine Your Assumptions

Write your assumptions regarding "one right-way thinking" and the value of generating many methods to achieve a goal or solve a problem, stating them as succinctly and powerfully as possible. For instance, you may believe "For most school improvement goals there is a right way to achieve success and it can be found in educational research." Share your assumptions with colleagues in the spirit of dialogue.

_____

_____

_____

_____

_____

_____

Deepen Your Understanding

Describe your experiences with brainstorming and with other methods of generating ideas. Discuss methods you have used for selecting the most promising approaches from initial lists of ideas. For example, you may recall the generation of ideas that occurred as you selected strategies to use in your school or district improvement efforts, or you may consider a personal experience such as identifying places to visit or activities for a family vacation.

_____

_____

_____

_____

_____

_____

ENGAGE IN NEXT ACTION THINKING

Specify actions you will take to identify multiple pathways to achieve a goal, the methods you will use to select the most powerful approaches, and by what dates you will take those actions.

_____

_____

_____

_____

_____

_____

CHAPTER 6

Promote Breakthrough Thinking

If you want to achieve the significant change that you and others need, you must achieve a paradigm shift in thinking.

—Gerald Nadler &
Shozo Hibino

Breakthrough innovations depend on ordinary people, bridging their expertise and building communities around their insights.

—Kathleen Eisenhardt

My assumptions: Breakthrough thinking is a powerful source of energy and innovation. Breakthroughs can be cultivated through dialogue and other forms of interaction that recognize and appreciate diverse experiences and perspectives.

"Breakthrough thinking" is a change in view regarding a particular subject after which everything related to that subject is viewed in a fresh and more empowering way. David Perkins (2000) in *The Eureka Effect: The Art and Logic of Breakthrough Thinking* says breakthrough thinking is creativity that makes a decisive break with the past in a way that is transformative rather than incremental.

As mentioned in this book's introductory chapter, in *The Right Words at the Right Time*, Marlo Thomas (2002) offers director Mike Nichols's description of breakthroughs in his life: "Two or three times in my life I have read or heard something that seemed in a moment to change me so palpably that I actually heard or felt a click, a sound, tumblers falling into place. . . . [I]t is simply the experience of becoming somebody slightly different, somebody new, the next you" (p. 238).

Thomas also provides Paul McCartney's account of the origins of his well-known song, "Let It Be," which he wrote in 1968 during a troubled time in his life. One night his mother, Mary, who had died many years before, came to him in a dream and said to him "very gently, very reassuringly, 'Let it be.' It was lovely," McCartney wrote of the experience. "I woke up with a great feeling. It was really like she had visited me at this very difficult point in my life and gave me this message: Be gentle, don't fight things, just try and go with the flow and it will all work out" (p. 218).

> [A] breakthrough idea seldom occurs instantaneously as a bolt out of the blue. Breakthrough ideas occur when the mind has been prepared, stimulated, and opened to the possibilities.
>
> —Gerald Nadler & Shozo Hibino

Breakthroughs may seem to occur in an instant with what Perkins calls a "cognitive snap," although preparation for them often takes a very long time and occurs after an accumulation of experience and knowledge. For instance, a superintendent tells about hearing statistics regarding the large number of young men of color in prison and has a breakthrough thought that learning to read is a matter of life and death for many students. Teachers describe epiphanies that occurred when students learned things the teachers did not believe they could learn, seemingly realizing in that instant that their students were capable of more than they had previously thought.

> [T]o solve the problems we confront, and for the human species to advance—quite possibly to survive—we are now called upon fundamentally and radically to change our minds, to change our way of thinking and seeing, to bridge the gap between our knowledge and our values.
>
> —Gerald Nadler & Shozo Hibino

Breakthroughs may have many sources. Andrew Hargadon (2003) in *How Breakthroughs Happen: The Surprising Truth About How Companies Innovate* cites the value of networks or "collectives" to provide a range of perspective and ideas and to offer emotional support to innovators whose work goes against the established ways of doing things. "[C]ollectives encourage individuals to think different, together," Hargadon writes. "When you work with others who are visibly engaged in and passionate about the work, you feel better about it yourself" (p. 107). He quotes a manager of an engineering group who said, "There are cases where the person who has the knowledge is sitting right next to you and it goes unnoticed and you plow a lot of ground you didn't necessarily have to" (p. 165).

A potent form of preparation for breakthroughs, from my experience, is dialogue with others whose authentic views offer a stark contradiction to some of our most strongly held perspectives, explanations, and assumptions. Another form of preparation is the intellectual engagement involved in developing a clearly articulated purpose and a richly detailed vision. Consequently, leaders who assist staff members in gaining clarity about their purposes and vision of what they wish to create and who frequently engage them in dialogue lay the foundation for breakthrough thinking and innovation.

> I don't have any ambitions other than to change the way people think.
>
> —Clay Christensen

EXAMINE YOUR ASSUMPTIONS

Write your assumptions regarding breakthrough thinking, stating them as succinctly and powerfully as possible. For instance, you may believe that "Breakthrough thinking is so random and rare it really doesn't have any relevance to the daily work of improving teaching and learning." Share your assumptions with colleagues in the spirit of dialogue.

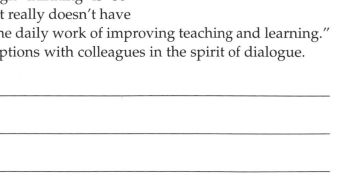

> There is nothing more powerful than an idea whose time has come.
>
> —Victor Hugo

_____

_____

_____

_____

_____

_____

DEEPEN YOUR UNDERSTANDING

Describe breakthroughs you have experienced, the events or experiences that led to the breakthroughs, and the effects they had on your personal or professional lives. For example, you may recall "aha" moments or epiphanies related to a challenging subject that you were studying, a new way of teaching a difficult concept, or sudden insight into a student's view of a lesson or classroom behavioral problem. Discuss ways that breakthroughs might be stimulated in your school or organization.

_____

_____

_____

_____

_____

_____

ENGAGE IN NEXT ACTION THINKING

Specify actions you will take to stimulate individual or collective breakthrough thinking and by what date.

_____

_____

_____

_____

_____

_____

REFERENCES

Hargadon, A. (2003). *How breakthroughs happen: The surprising truth about how companies innovate.* Boston: Harvard Business School Press.

Perkins, D. (2000). *The eureka effect: The art and logic of breakthrough thinking.* New York: W. W. Norton.

Thomas, M. (2002). *The right words at the right time.* New York: Atria Books.

CHAPTER 7

Develop a Theory of Action and Use Storytelling to Communicate It

Every school improvement program reflects beliefs and assumptions about how students learn, how schools should be run, and how change takes place. . . . Taken together, these beliefs and assumptions constitute a program's or organization's 'theories of action'—implicit and explicit understandings of how a school or program can accomplish its goals. . . . [W]hile many schools have goals, mission statements, and strategic plans, few have clearly articulated or well-examined theories of action.

—Thomas Hatch

We are defined by our stories, which continually form us and make us vital and give us hope.

—Max DePree

> **My assumptions: Improvement efforts are shaped by theories of action, whether or not we are aware of them. Leaders who develop and communicate clear, coherent, and compelling theories of action through stories and other means are more likely to produce the results they desire.**

Think of a theory of action as a set of underlying assumptions about how the organization will move from its current state to its desired future. A theory of action lays out for examination each of the links in a chain of causal events and the underlying assumptions that support them. We decide to do "x" because we believe "y." For instance, we may reduce class size in the primary grades because we believe students will benefit academically and socially in such settings.

These assumptions affect improvement efforts whether they are hidden from us because we have never consciously considered them or are explicit because we have thoughtfully reflected upon their efficacy and articulated them to others. Even if unarticulated, our current theories of action can sometimes be inferred from actions we take to achieve our goals. For example, an elementary school's primary strategy to improve student reading may be the creation of a parent newsletter devoted to tips on improving literacy at home. An inference about the school's theory of action might be that reading will improve for all or most students because (1) parent engagement is the most effective means to improve reading performance, (2) the strategies contained within the newsletter are sufficiently powerful that if used in the home they will improve reading, (3) all or most parents will read the newsletter, (4) parents who have read the newsletter will understand what it asks them to do, and (5) parents will apply what they have learned with sufficient consistency that reading will improve. This is, of course, a simplified example. But many schools use one or more relatively weak interventions to pursue substantial goals and have theories of action that would not survive professional scrutiny if they were surfaced and discussed.

> The telling of stories leads to shared meaning and emotional experience that changes something profoundly.
>
> —John Kao

> The universal love of stories is not a coincidence; our brains function by constructing narratives. Adults and children alike live, learn, and relate to others through stories. Unlike other forms of writing, stories engage our emotions and imagination in the process of learning.
>
> —Editors of *American Educator*

Once school leaders and teachers have a theory of action that is sufficiently robust to produce the desired result, that theory must be repeatedly shared in many places over a long period to motivate and guide improvement efforts. Communication may include letters to staff members and parents brief remarks at the beginning of various

> The universe is made of stories, not atoms.
>
> —Muriel Rukeyser

meetings, or explanations provided that establish a context and rationale for professional learning.

Stories provide a powerful means by which a theory of action can be simply explained and put in human terms. They can help educators, parents, and community members understand why change is important or why particular approaches were selected.

> Progress cannot happen without a good narrative.
>
> —Paul Danos

> I decided we would tell stories in our company. We'd tell stories about our goals and objectives, stories that would explain our core values and our vision of the future, and stories that would celebrate our victories. We'd even share a few stories that would underscore what should be done.
>
> —David Armstrong

Stories can provide a plotline and characters with whom listeners can relate. Leaders can use stories about school traditions or individual students, for example, to articulate the school's goals and to link the old with the new. Stories provide a means by which leaders can explain or reinterpret the past, use the past as a stimulus for new action, and illuminate a path for the future. Such stories may be large in scope, or broken into smaller pieces to illustrate particular ideas or perspectives.

EXAMINE YOUR ASSUMPTIONS

Write your assumptions regarding the value of theories of action in understanding and articulating a school's approach to improvement, stating them as succinctly and powerfully as possible. For instance, you may believe that "A theory of action complicates and impedes improvement because it's clear to everyone what has to be done and why it must be done." Share your assumptions with colleagues in the spirit of dialogue.

_____

_____

_____

_____

_____

_____

_____

_____

_____

_____

Deepen Your Understanding

To better understand the power of stories to shape behavior, discuss the influence stories have had on your motivation and action (these stories may have had either a positive or negative effect), particularly stories linked to school traditions and students. For example, you might recall stories that are frequently told in your school or district, stories told in your own family regarding various relatives, or stories that coaches, religious leaders, or political figures have told that influenced your thinking and actions.

_____

_____

_____

_____

_____

_____

_____

_____

_____

ENGAGE IN NEXT ACTION THINKING

Specify actions you will take to clarify and communicate the theory (or theories) of action that guides your work as an educational leader (particularly those connected to major school improvement initiatives) and by what date you will take those actions.

_____

_____

_____

_____

_____

_____

_____

_____

_____

_____

CHAPTER 8

Gain Clarity Through Writing, Speaking, and Reflecting on Action

[C]larity and focus describe the most basic predisposition of authentic leaders: they know what they want, and they pursue it. . . . [T]hey prefer directness and specificity in their dealings with constituents about these goals, and they exemplify their commitment in their behavior.

—Robert Evans

Creating your future involves a continuous cycle of reflection and action. By taking action, you find out which aspects of your vision, goals, and plans are workable and which can be refined.

—Dave Ellis

> **My assumptions: Clarity of thought is a powerful enabling force. Writing, speaking, and reflecting on our actions are potent means for achieving clarity. In addition, speaking to a committed listener bestows clarity as it assists us in cutting through the fog-like nature of thoughts that often occupy our minds.**

While there are many ways to clarify our thinking, in this chapter I recommend three in particular: writing, speaking, and reflecting on our actions. Combining two or three of these processes adds additional benefit. These methods help us better understand and express our purposes, values, intentions, assumptions, and theories of action for the purpose of creating the results we most desire.

Writing is a way of freezing our thinking, of slowing down the thoughts that pass through our consciousness at lightning speed, so we can examine our views and alter them if appropriate. Writing enables us to note inconsistencies, logical flaws, and areas that would benefit from additional clarity. I recommend writing progressively shorter and shorter drafts to crystallize and succinctly express key intentions and beliefs so they can be powerfully stated in a sentence or two.

> An individual's consciousness forms only in literacy. . . . Reading and writing radically alter perception.
>
> —Barry Sanders

Speaking—even out loud to ourselves or into a voice recorder—also aids understanding and clarity. I often am not sure what I think about a subject until I have heard myself speak about it. After talking about a subject I may think to myself, "Yes, that's exactly right" or "That's not it at all" or "This part of what I said is clear but this other part is still confusing to me." And then I modify my speaking to reflect my new understanding.

Speaking as a means of clarification is significantly enhanced when we do so in the presence of a committed listener who simply hears us without judgment or his or her own agenda. Feeling truly heard and accepted by another person is a powerful experience, and clarity regarding our purposes, values, fundamental choices, intentions, theories of action, and assumptions is increased when we speak about these things to someone who encourages the full expression of our thinking in a nondirective, nonjudgmental way. Being in the presence of someone who has no purpose other than to absorb our thoughts and feelings and to deeply understand our meaning is a rare and often unforgettable event.

> People learn best through active involvement and through thinking about and becoming articulate about what they have learned.
>
> —Ann Lieberman

I encourage you to seek out individuals who will listen carefully, honor your intentions, and who will speak only for the purpose of clarifying something that is not understood or to encourage you to continue speaking. I cannot overemphasize the importance of open-ended, nonjudgmental listening as a way to clarify your purposes, values, and assumptions; add specificity to your goals; and to identify alternative ways to achieve those goals. I will have more to say on this subject in Chapter 11.

Another way to gain clarity is to try a promising behavior or practice and to reflect on its effectiveness. Sometimes it is important to move off the fence of indecision and make a tentative commitment to a course of action. And it is equally important that we pause frequently to see if it is producing the results we desire, or at least an initial approximation of those results. Writing and speaking are wonderful means for such reflection because they externalize our views so we can truly encounter them.

EXAMINE YOUR ASSUMPTIONS

Write your assumptions regarding clarity of thought as an enabling force for leaders, stating them as succinctly and powerfully as possible. For instance, you may believe "It's not my job to be clear. I say whatever is on my mind and it is the responsibility of others to make sense of it." Share your assumptions with colleagues in the spirit of dialogue.

_____

_____

_____

_____

_____

_____

DEEPEN YOUR UNDERSTANDING

Describe the methods you find most effective in clarifying your thinking. Discuss the benefits you receive from that clarity. For example, consider ways in which you use writing (for instance, journal keeping), discussion with others, interacting with ideas of experts through reading, or other approaches to clarify your views.

_____

_____

_____

_____

_____

_____

_____

ENGAGE IN NEXT ACTION THINKING

Specify actions you will take to clarify your views on important subjects that are now at hand and by what date you will take those actions.

_____

_____

_____

_____

_____

_____

_____

PART II

Transformation Through Interpersonal Influence

Change the world—one conversation at a time. . . . It is not enough to be willing to speak. The time has come for you to speak. . . . Your time of holding back, of guarding your private thoughts, is over. Your function in life is to make a declarative statement.

—Susan Scott

Well-expressed ideas and observations can shift consciousness and change life's prospects.

—John R. O'Neil

The language leaders use and the ways in which they interact with others can disempower or empower, enable or disable, intensify resistance or increase commitment, and inspire passion and creativity or promote resignation and passivity. Here's an example: One evening a few years back I sat for dinner with several educational leaders who had asked me to speak the next day about professional learning to a group of area educators. In between their exchanges of information about upcoming events or projects in which they were engaged, individuals would speak at some length with anger and frustration about decisions by the state legislature, the governor, or the state education agency. As dinner progressed, one person's observations seemed only to intensify the frustration of the next speaker. Without quite being aware why, I awoke the next morning feeling discouraged and resigned about any sort of improvement in teaching and learning, let alone the type of dramatic changes I would advocate that day. As I thought back on the previous evening's conversation, I realized the language of complaint and resignation is indeed contagious and can deaden the human spirit and lead to organizational atrophy.

> **A basic premise of this book is that high-quality relationships built upon clarity, directness, and integrity compel change and produce results. To that end, the chapters in this section address the importance of candor, of making and keeping promises, of committed listening, of dialogue, and of making specific, actionable requests, among other topics.**

When educators speak with clarity, possibility, and accountability, and when they interact with others in respectful and mutually satisfying ways, they empower themselves and their organizations to produce extraordinary results. Such interactions add purpose, joy, and energy to our lives and the lives of those with whom we relate and increase the organization's capacity to engage in demanding, complex tasks and to sustain that effort over time.

CHAPTER 9

Tell Your Truth

What you perceive, your observations, feelings, interpretations, are all your truth. Your truth is important. Yet it is not The Truth. . . . When you accept responsibility for your thinking, you can speak without pushing your truth at the other person and minimize defensive responses. Chances are, people will listen more closely to what you say if you first acknowledge that it is your perception and may not be shared by anyone else.

—Linda Ellinor & Glenna Gerard

I wonder how many children's lives might be saved if we educators disclosed what we know to each other.

—Roland Barth

civility

> **My assumptions: We generate energy to create the results we desire when we consistently speak our truth forthrightly and with compassion. While telling our truth may be difficult in the short term, other people have the capacity to receive and benefit from it.**

The perspective of this chapter can be put quite simply: Be candid. Tell "your truth." And, if necessary, tell it again and again to improve relationships and achieve intended results. Candid communication may be called "uncompromising straight talk," "courageous conversation," "entering the danger," or "fierce conversation." Whatever term is used, it means nonjudgmentally describing what we observe from our vantage point, stating our assumptions, and making clear, actionable requests for what we want. While it is common to feel fear or anxiety when expressing our views, hence "entering the danger," withholding them is often the difference between actions that benefit students and those that do not. When we express this truth, we feel energized, vital, and more effective.

> Words are a form of action, capable of influencing change.
>
> —Ingrid Bengis

Avoiding telling the truth in schools is so pervasive in many schools that educators have coined a term to describe it—"parking lot meetings." Such truth-telling occurs when individuals gather in parking lots, hallways, or bathrooms during or after meetings to say what is really on their minds. As a result, many schools are "pseudo-communities" based on "contrived collegiality" rather than places that foster authentic exchange of views for the benefit of students.

Few claims are based in "absolute truth" (truth with a capital "T"). Rather, human beings formulate "their truth" (truth with a lowercase "t") from experiences and assumptions that have shaped their perception of "reality."

Summoning courage to offer our truth enables us as leaders, no matter what our formal position in the organization, to achieve results that are aligned with our values, purposes, and intentions. In addition, truth-telling enlivens our relationships and adds vitality to our work. It is an antidote to the boredom that too frequently permeates meetings and other professional interactions and the "slow death spiral" that too many educators experience in their work lives.

We have many reasons for withholding our truth in professional settings, some of which are quite valid. Few individuals are rewarded for sharing comments that increase anxiety or conflict and that introduce complications and messiness where once there was clarity and certainty. Having anger directed at us because of our views can be unpleasant. And feeling ostracized by colleagues for taking unpopular positions is often painful.

> Tell the truth about what you want in life and what you're willing to do to get it. Being candid releases the energy that's bound up in hiding the truth from others and ourselves.
>
> —Dave Ellis

Educational leaders want their schools to be well regarded, so there is a natural tendency to refrain from saying things that may place themselves or their organization in an unflattering light. In addition, speaking our truth may not alter the outcome, and in a few situations, it may even put our career prospects or jobs at risk. Superintendents have lost their jobs because they told the truth about a problem and the barriers that impeded its resolution.

Telling the truth, even with data at your side, about achievement problems related to race, social class, and gender is fraught with risks. In these situations, I encourage you to carefully consider the costs and benefits of various courses of action; as in all such situations, there typically is no single correct way to proceed.

> I believe the health of an organization is inversely proportional to the number of its nondiscussables: the fewer the nondiscussables, the healthier the culture; the more the nondiscussables, the sicker it is.
>
> —Roland Barth

Given those caveats, truth-telling can nonetheless help us gain clarity about our views, be an important source of learning for others, and deepen relationships with colleagues, an important aspect of job satisfaction and the retention of teachers in their schools. Telling our truth may also lead to "breakthroughs" for others. When our truth resonates with the truth that others experience, it can have a very powerful effect on a group's intentions and actions. In addition, withholding our perspective, particularly our emotions, is a barrier to tapping our inherent creative and problem-solving abilities.

> The great sadness of denying truth is that we all become accomplices in our own spiritual demise.
>
> —Max DePree

Prefacing "our truth" with "this is what I hold to be true" or "this is how I see it" or a similar phrase recognizes the legitimacy of others' points of view. Inviting others to share their views in the accepting and inquiring spirit of dialogue reduces defensiveness, improves relationships, and often leads to new understanding and clarity regarding next steps. More will be said about dialogue in Chapter 10.

EXAMINE YOUR ASSUMPTIONS

Write your assumptions regarding professional candor, stating them as succinctly and powerfully as possible. For instance, you may believe "Candor seldom produces desirable results and is usually not worth the risk." Share your assumptions with colleagues in the spirit of dialogue.

_____

_____

_____

_____

_____

_____

_____

_____

_____

_____

Deepen Your Understanding

Recall times when you were candid with others and describe the effect on you (emotionally and physically) and on others. Discuss approaches to speaking candidly that increase the likelihood of a positive outcome.

_____

_____

_____

_____

_____

_____

_____

_____

ENGAGE IN NEXT ACTION THINKING

Identify a relatively low-risk situation in which you can state your views. Rehearse what you might say, including your observations and assumptions. Consider making a request if that is appropriate.

_____

_____

_____

_____

_____

_____

_____

_____

_____

_____

CHAPTER 10

Use Genuine Dialogue

Out beyond the idea of right thinking and wrong thinking is a field. . . . I will meet you there.

—Jalaluddin Rumi

Engaging in dialogue once, twice, or a handful of times will yield more meaningful conversation around important questions. If practiced on a continuing basis, it can produce significant shifts in the culture of the group or organization.

—Linda Ellinor & Glenna Gerard

> **My assumptions: Our beliefs and those of others have a powerful effect on professional practice. Dialogue engages us in a thorough examination of our beliefs, deepens our understanding, and improves relationships.**

Lectures, publications, and traditional training methods used to improve teaching and leadership are usually insufficient to affect practice unless they are preceded or accompanied by genuine dialogue. While acquiring knowledge and developing skills are important, some of the most profound changes in individuals occur at the level of beliefs and assumptions.

Each of us operates from a set of beliefs and images about how the world works that derive from our experiences. While often unknown to us, these "mental models" exert significant influence over our professional practices. Some of these implicit beliefs unknowingly impede progress toward our goals. A part of us—our intentions—wants to go in one direction. Another part of us—our beliefs—may act as a brake that slows our progress.

Dialogue is the process by which we make known to one another the assumptions that underlie our perspectives and the thought processes and information that shape those assumptions. These underlying factors may include, for instance, other layers of assumptions, learning gleaned from life experiences, or findings of scientific studies. Dialogue can build bridges of understanding, clarify areas of agreement and disagreement, promote deeper understanding of issues, and improve a group's capacity to make good decisions. In addition, when we remain open to the perspectives of others in the spirit of inquiry, we may change our views in ways that support our most important goals.

> It is hard to overemphasize the importance of an ongoing practice of dialogue to the maturing of conversations that will bear the fruits of learning and transformation.
>
> —Linda Ellinor & Glenna Gerard

In *Dialogue: Rediscover the Transforming Power of Conversation*, Linda Ellinor and Glenna Gerard (1998) list several qualities of genuine dialogue: suspension of judgment, release of our need for a specific outcome, an inquiry into and examination of underlying assumptions, authenticity, a slower pace of interaction with silence between speakers, and listening deeply to self and others for collective meaning. To those ends, they suggest focusing on shared meaning and learning, listening without resistance, respecting differences, suspending role and status distinctions, sharing responsibility and leadership, and speaking to the group as a whole (one-on-one conversations in front of a group lead to the disengagement of other group members).

> To achieve different results, we must take different actions. Because our actions are shaped by how we see the world, to do something different we must see something different. We must question the assumptions and mental models we use to see the world, frame our thinking, and determine action. Innovation depends on it.
>
> —M. Kathryn Clubb

Dialogue is distinct from discussion, debate, and argument. Advocacy for a point of view is not part of dialogue, nor is attempting to convince others that they are wrong. While each of these methods sometimes have their place, they often produce defensiveness, which is a barrier to the deep understanding and transformational learning that often accompanies dialogue. The assumptions we hold as unquestionable "Truth" often represent some of the most fruitful areas for dialogue because alterations in these assumptions can produce profound changes in our lives.

EXAMINE YOUR ASSUMPTIONS

Write your assumptions regarding the value of dialogue in affecting beliefs, deepening understanding, and improving relationships, stating them as succinctly and powerfully as possible. For instance, you may believe "Change involves changing what we do, and it's more important to talk about what those actions will be than it is to engage in dialogue about our assumptions." Share your assumptions with colleagues in the spirit of dialogue.

_____

_____

_____

_____

_____

_____

_____

DEEPEN YOUR UNDERSTANDING

Consider the professional discussions in which you regularly participate to determine which ones would most benefit from dialogue. Describe ways that participants could learn the skills of dialogue and the methods that could be used to prevent the conversation from unintentionally shifting to debate, argument, or action planning.

_____

_____

_____

_____

_____

ENGAGE IN NEXT ACTION THINKING

The development of the skills of dialogue requires intention, practice, feedback, and persistence.

- Practice empathy in all conversations. Offer "gestures of empathy" to demonstrate that you see the world from another's perspective when you feel at an impasse with someone.
- Identify underlying assumptions in what you read and in what others say. Reflect on your own assumptions about that particular topic and consider how you would express them.
- Practice being nonjudgmental regarding your assumptions and those of others. Hold your assumptions loosely rather than as "the truth."

Specify which of these actions or others you will take and by what date.

_____

_____

_____

_____

_____

_____

_____

REFERENCE

Ellinor, L., & Gerard, G. (1998). *Dialogue: Rediscovering the transforming power of conversation.* New York: John Wiley & Sons.

CHAPTER 11

Listen to Others in a Deep, Committed Way

It seems so simple, but to be able to deeply listen to another without trying to fix, but to just be there with them, it is transformational in itself.

—Linda Ellinor & Glenna Gerard

While no single conversation is guaranteed to transform a company, a relationship, or a life, any single conversation can. Speak and listen as if this is the most important conversation you will ever have with this person.

—Susan Scott

> **My assumptions: Committed listening transforms relationships and deepens learning. Its skillful use requires practice and discipline.**

Dialogue and the other methods for transforming conversation discussed in this book have at their core a quality of listening that is rare in most human communication. This type of listening allows the speaker to determine the agenda for what is said, seeks to understand the speaker's views, is nonjudgmental, and honors the speaker's perspective. Because it is so rare and powerful, I believe it is one of the greatest gifts one human being can give another.

As someone with graduate degrees in counseling, I was taught "active listening"—to paraphrase the speaker's views and to reflect back his or her feelings. I asked questions that probed beneath the surface of what was said and assessed others' "needs" based on what they told me. Likewise, many of us have learned to demonstrate interest in what others are saying by asking questions, sharing our experiences related to what the speaker has said, and offering another perspective regarding the speaker's views.

In recent years, though, I have learned a different style of listening that I view as even more effective in helping others express their feelings and in clarifying their intentions and assumptions. Committed listening asks that I give my complete attention

> One of the greatest gifts you can give another human being is to care enough to listen to their story.
>
> —Richard Leider

to what the speaker is saying by removing distractions that are occurring around me (for instance, other tasks that I may not have fully set aside) and within me (things I want to say that are prompted by what the speaker has said). As a committed listener:

- I listen carefully to what is said without interruption until the person is finished, refraining from comment, commiseration, and offering assistance. And when the person seems to be done, I inquire, "What else?" to make certain he or she has spoken fully on the subject at hand.
- I convey nonverbally my full attention and interest in what is being said.
- I minimize my use of statements or questions that direct the conversations or subtly convey a point of view. I have learned to trust that people will reveal to me as little or as much as is appropriate at the moment. Even clarifying questions may take the conversation in a different direction than the one of greatest value to the speaker, so I use them sparingly. Likewise, knowing that I will say very little means that I will not use part of my attention to formulate a story I would like to tell about the subject at hand or to offer my interpretation of events.

> Listening is the doorway through which we allow the world to enter. How we listen, to what and to whom we listen, and the assumptions we listen through all frame our perceptions of reality. Listening may be the single most powerful act we perform; we listen and create reality based on what we hear in each moment.
>
> —Linda Ellinor & Glenna Gerard

- I genuinely honor the speaker's views even though they may not be my own. I typically make only a brief statement that conveys my understanding and nonjudgmental acceptance of what was said. Honoring a speaker's view is not the same as agreeing with what was said; disagreements about factual issues or differing views may be expressed later after the person has had an opportunity to speak his or her mind without interruption or can be deferred to another occasion. It is my experience that change is accelerated when someone feels the unconditional regard of another and as conversations focus on intention rather than contention. Contrarily, criticism promotes defensiveness, which in turn helps preserve the status quo.

> The people I have met who are most effective at changing the world have two qualities. On the one hand, they are extraordinarily committed, body and soul, to the change they want to see in the work, to a goal larger than themselves. On the other hand, they are extraordinarily open to listening to what is happening in the world, in others, and in themselves.
>
> —Adam Kahane

- I realize that when I find myself arguing with the person about our respective points of view I have slipped from committed listening to a form of interaction that is far more likely to produce heat than light. I then turn from sending communication and begin receiving again.
- I refrain from analyzing what has been said and why it is being said so that my mind is fully engaged with and respectful of the person's perspective.

While committed listening may sound simple, it is a demanding skill that requires practice and discipline in its execution. Without constant vigilance, it is easy to backslide into inattention, to redirect the speaker to better serve our interests, or to fall into argument or debate rather than provide genuine acceptance.

EXAMINE YOUR ASSUMPTIONS

Write your assumptions regarding the value of committed listening in high-quality relationships. For instance, you may believe "While listening is important, there simply isn't time in schools to give sustained attention to anyone." Share your assumptions with colleagues in the spirit of dialogue.

_____

_____

_____

_____

_____

_____

_____

_____

_____

DEEPEN YOUR UNDERSTANDING

Recall times when you were the recipient of exceptionally high-quality listening. Discuss the attributes of the interaction that you believe made it so memorable.

_____

_____

_____

_____

_____

_____

_____

_____

ENGAGE IN NEXT ACTION THINKING

Practice listening with your full attention to another person who is speaking about something of importance to him or her. Refrain from interrupting or asking questions. Convey your close attention through your body language and overall demeanor. Specify with whom you will do so and by what date.

CHAPTER 12

Make Requests to Initiate Action and Create Results

Self-responsible human beings are "request machines." They know that one way to get what they want is to ask for it.

—Dave Ellis

We must change the way we speak, the way we ask, the way we listen.

—Susan Scott

> **My assumptions: We are more likely to get what we want when we ask for it clearly and directly. Requests produce results when they are specific, actionable, and have a deadline by which they will be honored.**

larity regarding intentions (what we want to create) provides focus and energy for creating the results we desire. Clearly expressed intentions guide individual and collective action. But simply stating a desire for a particular outcome is not the same as asking one or more people to take specific actions related to that intention. We are far more likely to get things we want if we clearly and directly ask for them, and people are more likely to be motivated to give us what we want if they perceive it as a request (it's okay to say "no") rather than a demand (saying "no" leads to a negative consequence). Confusing requests and demands can strain relationships and inhibit the achievement of results.

A request is a statement of what we want someone to do that is actionable on his or her part and allows the individual to turn down the request without a negative consequence. Individuals may accept, decline, or defer a decision until a specified time. While the word "request" may or may not be used, it is important the recipient of the request understand that a response is sought and that agreeing to the request is considered a promise between the two parties.

> If you're leading without authority, other people's attention spans are going to be short whenever you try to communicate with them. Forget two-hour speeches—most people aren't willing to give you more than 30 seconds! So you have to use their attention wisely. You have to make your interventions short, simple, intelligible, and relevant.
>
> —Ronald Heifetz

Think of "stretch goals" or other large-scale intentions as bundles of requests that may eventually be made at different levels of complexity and specificity to various individuals. For instance, a superintendent may want quality professional learning to be part of teachers' daily work life within three years. As a result, she might ask principals to read the *National Staff Development Council's Standards for Staff Development* and be prepared to discuss its implications at the next principals' meeting. (If it truly is a request, an individual may decline.) The superintendent might also ask the district's assistant superintendent

> You have to know how to have what I call "conversations for action." Everybody spends time in meetings where there's a lot of talk and not a lot of action. That's because we don't identify which kinds of conversations result in performance.
>
> —Raymona Sharpnack

for instruction to work with principals and teacher leaders to design school schedules so that every teacher will be part of a team that meets several times a week. During team meetings, teachers will work together to improve their lessons, to help one another more deeply understand the content they are teaching, and to examine student work and other evidence to determine the effectiveness of their lessons. The assistant superintendent might, in turn, make requests of several teachers to attend a workshop offered by the local university on the use of protocols for examining student work and to present their views on this method to a districtwide committee.

Requests provide a helpful alternative to giving advice and using obligatory language. Rather than telling others what they *should* do, *must* do, or *need* to do (all of which can produce defensive responses and dampen motivation), leaders can state their intentions and make requests. We may also say our assumptions about the subject under discussion and invite the other person to do the same in the spirit of dialogue. Chapter 15 discusses the drawbacks of obligatory language.

Persistence in making requests is often important. In some circumstances, it may be necessary to ask for what we want several times over a period of weeks, months, or even years before a request is granted. And even if the request is never granted, persistence may represent an important way to stand up for one's values and views and stimulate in others important professional learning.

EXAMINE YOUR ASSUMPTIONS

Write your assumptions regarding the value of making requests as a tool for realizing your goals. For instance, you may believe "If something is important, people should know what to do. Therefore, asking them to do it is unnecessary." Share your assumptions with colleagues in the spirit of dialogue.

_____

_____

_____

_____

_____

_____

_____

DEEPEN YOUR UNDERSTANDING

Describe times when you or others have confused requests with demands and the consequences of that confusion. Discuss ways that you can make requests without producing unintended negative consequences.

_____

_____

_____

_____

_____

_____

_____

Engage in Next Action Thinking

Practice identifying requests that will contribute to achieving what you desire. Write out one or more requests, making certain they are indeed requests (not demands) and that they are actionable by the person to whom you are making the request.

_____

_____

_____

_____

_____

_____

CHAPTER 13

Make and Keep Promises

We define integrity—a key ingredient in character and a primary spiritual muscle—as doing what you say you are going to do when you say you are going to do it.

—Jim Loehr & Tony Schwartz

Only one thing is more toxic and destructive than a promise made and not kept: a pattern of promises made and not kept.

—Roland Barth

My assumptions: Promises are the starting points of action. They keep us on track for realizing our intentions. Making and keeping promises demonstrates integrity, promotes trust, and gets important work done. Internal accountability to one another—rather than external accountability through state testing or other methods—is the most powerful source of continuous improvement in teaching and learning.

Promises made and kept are the highest representations of our integrity—they are an affirmation of our desire to behave consistently with our stated values and purposes. Without commitment to sustained, purposeful action and accountability for those actions, schools are unlikely to achieve their intended outcomes. Because promises stimulate action, organizations realize more of their intentions when individuals within them make and keep promises and expect others to do the same. Consequently, organizations are ultimately only as effective as the promises made and kept by the individuals within them.

When promises are not explicitly stated, much of their value may be lost. A *New Yorker* cartoon (Jan. 7, 2002, p. 55) shows two men sitting at a bar. One says to the other: "Doris and I have an unspoken agreement, but she won't tell me what it is." Many people have unspoken agreements that one or more of the parties may not know exists. And when that happens, misunderstanding and even complete breakdowns in relationships can result.

> Our promises create our lives. Our promises give life to our purposes and goals. Our promises move us into action. . . . Life works to the degree we keep our promises.
>
> —Dave Ellis

Another way of thinking about the significance of promises is to consider the promises we make to ourselves as well as those made to others. When we make promises to ourselves—for instance, as leaders to spend more time in schools and classrooms—but fail to keep them, our own sense of personal efficacy is on the line even though we may be the only one who knows of the promise. And when we consistently let ourselves down in this way, a sense of resignation is almost certain to follow.

Knowing how to move into action and maintain momentum is a fundamental aspect of promise-keeping. In *Getting Things Done: The Art of Stress-Free Productivity*, David Allen (2001) stresses the importance of clearly defined outcomes and the value of knowing the next actions for moving them forward. "Next actions" are promises individuals make to others about what they agree to accomplish by a particular time. Without such a focus and a system of internal accountability for sustaining attention on goals and actions, organizations are far less likely to achieve their intended outcomes.

> I used to make a lot of them (agreements), just to win people's approval. When I realized the price I was paying on the back end for not keeping those agreements, I became a lot more conscious about the ones I made.
>
> —David Allen

A simple and common example of the value of making and keeping promises is attending meetings we have agreed to attend and, when we are responsible for meetings, beginning and ending them on time. When individuals hold their participation and the established beginning and ending times as promises, meetings are more productive and help establish a climate of responsibility throughout the organization.

A November 2001 *Fast Company* article about IBM's PC division head Bob Moffat provides an illustration of the value of "calendar integrity": "Moffat always shows up on time for meetings, a sign of accountability and respect for his colleagues that is almost unheard of at his level," the article points out. "Says one senior manager: 'We have a name for it here. It's called calendar integrity'"(Fishman, p. 96).

Because in many groups providing an excuse for not fulfilling a promise is regarded as the equivalent of having kept the promise, it is important to establish group agreements about promises—the protocol that will be followed when problems arise in the completion of a task that may mean that a promise will not be kept. For instance, district curriculum and instruction staff members might agree that promises are expected to be kept in the manner in which they are specified, and that if the person who has made the promise becomes aware of a problem, he or she will immediately notify others and renegotiate the agreement. Consistent breakdowns of promise-keeping by one or more people may signal that it is time to discuss the problem with individuals who are not honoring their agreements or to review group agreements and remind everyone why promise-keeping is important.

Examine Your Assumptions

Write your assumptions regarding the value of making and keeping promises, stating them as succinctly and powerfully as possible. For instance, you may believe "Given the number of balls that school leaders are asked to constantly juggle, it is unfair to expect people to honor their commitments or to even take the time to renegotiate them." Share your assumptions with colleagues in the spirit of dialogue.

_____

_____

_____

_____

_____

_____

DEEPEN YOUR UNDERSTANDING

Discuss the extent to which both promise-making and promise-keeping are norms in your organization. For example, consider whether individuals are expected to arrive on time for meetings and ways in which tardiness is addressed by leaders. If appropriate, consider ways that promise-making and promise-keeping might be addressed.

_____

_____

_____

_____

_____

_____

_____

NEXT ACTION THINKING

Create protocols for what will be done if unanticipated problems arise after an agreement is made. Specify who will take these actions and by what date.

_____

_____

_____

_____

_____

_____

REFERENCES

Allen, D. (2001). *Getting things done: The art of stress-free productivity.* New York: Viking.

Fishman, C. (2001, November). Leader—Bob Moffat. *Fast Company, 52,* 96.

The New Yorker. (2002, January 7). Cartoon. 55.

CHAPTER 14

Replace Questions With Declarative Statements

It is not enough to be willing to speak. The time has come for you to speak. . . . Your time of holding back, of guarding your private thoughts, is over. Your function in life is to make a declarative statement.

—Susan Scott

A chief event in life is the day in which we have encountered a mind that startled us.

—Emerson

My assumptions: Questions are often an indirect and less efficient method of stating assumptions and intentions, making requests, and deepening understanding. In addition, questions that are knowingly or unknowingly intended to elicit a particular answer often induce anxiety or defensiveness.

A teacher friend says she sometimes suffers from delusions of clarity. I have no such delusion as I approach the content of this chapter. When I interact with others about these ideas in face-to-face settings, it is quickly evident that my ideas about question-asking are confusing because they contradict recommendations made in numerous articles, courses, and workshops on teaching and leadership. We have been taught that effective leaders know how to use well-timed, thoughtfully articulated questions and that teachers' questioning strategies can stimulate students' interest, deepen understanding, and develop critical thinking skills.

Acknowledging that perspective, I ask you to approach this topic with an open mind and to thoughtfully consider situations in which declarative statements may better serve your purposes. I also ask you to consider how commonly used terms that connote questions, such as "inquiry" and "ask," make take on other meanings when viewed through the perspective of this chapter. For instance, the inquiry process may begin with an assertion or observation that startles us rather than with a question, and "ask" may take the form of a declarative statement that makes a request (for instance, the first two sentences in this paragraph). With that as context, I offer you the following reasons for reducing the number of questions you ask as a way to increase your interpersonal influence.

Educators sometimes disguise and dilute their points of view by asking questions rather than stating their observations, assumptions, intentions, and requests in simple, declarative sentences. While questions have merit when they are a method of genuine inquiry into the unknown, the unthinking use of questions is often a barrier to effective communication and deeper understanding.

Questions can dilute conversations in a number of ways. I have observed that people are often more comfortable asking a question than making a direct statement of their views, even when their perspective is evident in the wording of their questions. I have attended many meetings in which unanswered questions were the dominant form of interaction. One question was followed by another and then another without anyone succinctly stating their perspective on the subject. There is safety in such confusion because questions can provide immunity from the criticism that speakers fear will follow their declarative statements.

Another problem is that questions are often asked by those with more power to those with less power—for example, parents to children, teachers to students, and bosses to subordinates. Individuals in these circumstances often report that they felt interrogated and that it was not acceptable to pose their own questions. Because answering the questions of more powerful individuals usually is not optional, such interactions often provoke defensiveness and anxiety rather than an honest exchange of views regarding the subject.

A third problem is that questions are often nothing more than concealed, indirect statements of the speaker's point of view or disguised requests for a particular action. For instance, "Don't you think . . . ?" "Have you ever considered . . . ?" "Why don't you try . . . ?" begin with an indirect statement of the speaker's point of view. Turning such questions into statements or requests

("I think . . . " "I assume . . ." and "I'm asking you to . . .") is more honest, direct, and likely to receive the desired response. Such an approach also moves the conversation into a more fertile exchange of perspectives and assumptions, which in turn deepens understanding and promotes transformational learning.

> We all have multiple sets of assumptions that act as lenses or filters for our perceptions. . . . The next time you find yourself with a vastly different interpretation of events than a colleague . . . reveal your own thinking process and ask about the other person's.
>
> —Linda Ellinor & Glenna Gerard

While some questions appear on the surface to be open-ended, it quickly becomes evident that the speaker is fishing for the "correct answer." These questions imply that there is a single correct answer or solution to the problem and the speaker knows the answer. A particularly damaging outcome of this type of interaction is that those to whom the questions are directed may shut down their minds and become resigned and dependent.

Yet another problem is when someone in the role of listener asks questions that divert a conversation away from the topics of most value to the speaker. At one level, the questions may seem to demonstrate interest in the speaker's views; at another level, they are an expression of what the question-asker wants to know, which may or may not be what the speaker wishes to discuss.

Most of these problems can be overcome, I believe, when speakers directly state their observations and assumptions and invite others to respond in the spirit of dialogue. Such dialogue, of course, is based on equality of status and a lack of coercion. In addition, I believe that it is more fruitful for speakers who want others to take a particular action to make requests rather than to conceal their purpose within questions. It is far more effective—and more honest—to ask for behavior in the form of a request than to ask a question that may or may not reveal the speaker's real intentions.

> We find comfort from those who agree with us, growth from those who do not.
>
> —Anon.

EXAMINE YOUR ASSUMPTIONS

Write your assumptions regarding the value and place of question-asking in deepening understanding, affecting beliefs, and producing results, stating them as succinctly and powerfully as possible. For instance, you may believe "Questions are a particularly effective way of interacting because they provide the freedom and opportunity to inquire together into complex problems." Share your assumptions with colleagues in the spirit of dialogue.

_____

_____

_____

_____

_____

_____

Deepen Your Understanding

Describe times when questions you have asked or that were asked of you were indirect expressions of assumptions or disguised requests for agreement or action. For example, recall questions you or others have asked that begin with phrases such as "Wouldn't you agree . . . ?" or "Don't you think . . . ?" Consider ways you could reframe questions into a statement of intention, assumption, or request. Ask others for feedback regarding the clarity of your reframed statements.

_____

_____

_____

_____

_____

ENGAGE IN NEXT ACTION THINKING

Monitor your use of questions and develop a new habit of conversation that is less dependent on questions and more oriented to direct expressions of observations, intentions, assumptions, and requests. Specify when you will begin and what methods you will use to monitor this change in your behavior.

_____

_____

_____

_____

_____

_____

_____

CHAPTER 15

Minimize the Language of Obligation

A common strategy in life is to take something that matters to you and translate it into a sense of obligation, so that you manipulate yourself into doing what you want to do anyway. . . . When your actions are based on obligation, it is very hard to determine what truly matters to you.

—Robert Fritz

We persuade, cajole, manipulate, and issue directives. Nothing changes.

—Susan Scott

> **My assumptions: Language forms affect energy and guide action. The language of obligation diminishes motivation and increases dependency. Language that asserts our observations, assumptions, and intentions is more direct and honest and increases energy to sustain effort over time.**

While "obligatory language"—words such as *should*, *ought*, *must*, and *need*—are common in everyday communication, the sense of obligation they convey often takes its toll on our individual and collective sense of energy, commitment, and responsibility. Obligatory language seldom reveals the intentions, assumptions, or reasoning upon which the obligation is based and directs us to unquestioningly act in accordance with someone else's rules or standards rather than our own.

Sometimes the observations, intentions, and assumptions that stand behind obligatory language are even unknown to the speaker who "inherited" them unquestioningly from others. Because the human mind has a tendency to turn desire, once experienced, into obligation (at first I did it because I wanted to; now I do it because I *should* continue to do something I enjoy), we can inadvertently diminish our passion and capacity to invent the means by which we will achieve our goals and to pursue those means over time.

> You can trust your desires. . . . [W]e can let go of struggle and self-discipline. We can get what we want by following our passions—not by following other people's desires, doing what we "should" do, doing what we have always done in the past, or following any other external pressures. Instead, we can trust our desires.
>
> —Dave Ellis

Obligatory language by its very nature implies certainty, a belief that there is only one right way to approach a given situation. It is often spoken in a manner that implies "truth" with a capital "T" rather than as an assumption spoken to stimulate dialogue or invention. "Shoulds" typically withhold the observations, assumptions, intentions, and requests that if directly expressed would enable the recipient to enter into the kind of conversation advocated in this book and to decide on an appropriate course of action. Because "shoulds" are seldom expressed as requests, which a person may decline without negative consequences, obligatory language diminishes an individual's sense of personal power and resourcefulness.

Obligatory language imposes the speaker's point of view or intention upon others as if there is no viable alternative. Sometimes its authority comes from an unquestioned nameless source ("They say you should . . ."). In addition, the speaker's desire to control may be so strong that he or she does not desire a dialogue nor want to make a request because of the risk that it may be denied. Consequently, obligatory language is often in reality a demand for which the speaker does not wish to assume responsibility.

> Obligation is a flimsy base for creativity, way down the list behind passion, courage, instinct, and the desire to do something great.
>
> —Twyla Tharp

When we accept the obligations imposed by others as our own, we live in obedience to solutions someone else has invented to problems that we may or may not perceive as our own. Recipients of obligatory language often sense at some level that their prerogatives for self-determination are being usurped by the speaker. While the speaker may view such language as an expression of friendship and caring—or perhaps even of a more highly developed expertise or wisdom—recipients are more often inclined to experience it as controlling, meddling, or micromanaging. Of even greater consequence, I believe, is when recipients of such high-pressured advice interpret it as a reflection of their inability to successfully conduct their own lives and surrender their capacity for self-management, increasingly turning to others for direction.

When used by "outsiders" (those who work in district offices, consultants, professors, and so on) who are attempting to affect school practices, obligatory language often leads teachers and principals to become dependent on "expert" advice (which is often spoken in obligatory terms), which in turn contributes to the resignation and dependency that many educators experience in their professional lives. And when teachers and principals use obligatory language to describe their motivation ("We should do . . ." rather than "We want to do . . ."), their sense of commitment and responsibility is diminished. In either case, the obligatory language of outsiders fosters dependency and reduces commitment.

EXAMINE YOUR ASSUMPTIONS

Write your assumptions regarding the use and effects of obligatory language, stating them as succinctly and powerfully as possible. For instance, you may believe "Obligatory language is an effective and efficient method to get people to do what we want and consequently is a valuable skill for producing results." Share your assumptions with colleagues in the spirit of dialogue.

DEEPEN YOUR UNDERSTANDING

Describe the effects on you when others tell you that you "must" or "need" to do something. For example, recall the common reaction of feeling disrespected or defensive in such situations. Practice identifying the intentions, assumptions, and requests that stand behind your obligatory language and that of others.

_____

_____

_____

_____

_____

_____

ENGAGE IN NEXT ACTION THINKING

Become conscious about your use of obligatory language. Ask someone to let you know when you are using it. Develop the habit of substituting statements of intentions, assumptions, and requests for obligatory language, using these statements as a springboard for dialogue. Pay attention to the results of this new habit. Specify exactly what actions you will take and by what date you will take those actions.

_____

_____

_____

_____

_____

_____

CHAPTER 16

Decrease the Use of Cause-Effect Language

In our minds, we think very simply in terms of cause. We think that one cause is enough to bring about what is there. With the practice of looking deeply, we find out that one cause can never be enough in order to bring about an effect.

—Thich Nhat Hanh

There is magic in being in the present in your life. I'm always amazed at the power of clear observation simply about what's going on, what's true.

—David Allen

> **My assumptions: The habitual use of cause-effect language to describe the influence that others have on our feelings and actions diminishes our sense of efficacy and our ability to produce the results we desire.**

Most of us use cause-effect language with little awareness of the effects it has on our sense of personal and professional efficacy and on the efficacy of others. For instance, we may say, "The principal upset me by what he said in the meeting today about how our school is not being successful with all its students." When we use language that attributes the source of our feelings and actions to others, we give others tremendous power over our lives and we lose a portion of our freedom. Consequently, such attributions often lead to feelings of powerlessness and resignation and diminish our capacity to produce the results we desire.

Because most of our feelings and reactions are a result of many factors, attributing causation to one particular thing is usually very difficult. Some social scientists use the term "overdetermined" to describe the complex set of factors that contribute to a particular result. When we say, "What you just said makes me angry," we are claiming the speaker's words are the sole and most important source of our feelings. While in some instances that may be true and while the person's words undoubtedly played a part in our reaction, any number of factors may also have affected our response. Our reaction to the principal's comments at a meeting, for instance, may be affected by significant but less proximal events that were not evident to us at the moment—a poor night's sleep, a family argument from the evening before, or even a tone of voice that reminds us of how a parent spoke to us as a child.

The most effective and accurate way to depict our feelings and reactions, I believe, is to simply report them without attribution of cause. Instead of saying "The principal made me angry," we might say "I am angry about what the principal said at the meeting" or "I find myself obsessing about the principal's comment that if teachers really cared about kids we'd be more open to new ideas."

Once acknowledged, we may choose to use our feelings to gain clarity regarding our observations, assumptions, and requests related to the situation. We might say to the principal, "Your view seems to be that teachers' resistance to new ideas is the major source of problems in this school *(Observation)*. I believe most teachers in this school want to do an outstanding job for kids *(Assumption)*. I'd like the entire faculty to have a genuine dialogue about their views on this subject, and I'm asking you to provide a generous amount of time for it at our next faculty meeting" *(Request)*.

EXAMINE YOUR ASSUMPTIONS

Write your assumptions regarding the effects of cause-effect language on personal and professional efficacy, stating them as succinctly and powerfully as possible. For instance, you may believe "A person's feelings and reactions are determined by what happens to them. Because he or she really has no choice in the matter, cause-effect language is an accurate depiction of reality." Share your assumptions with colleagues in the spirit of dialogue.

_____

_____

_____

_____

_____

_____

_____

_____

_____

_____

Deepen Your Understanding

Identify a recent situation in which you attributed your feelings or actions to others. For example, recall thinking or expressing phrases such as "Susan made me so mad during that meeting" or "The school board's decision last night really upsets me." Describe ways you might have responded differently by reporting an observation, offering an assumption in the spirit of dialogue, and making a request.

_____

_____

_____

_____

_____

_____

_____

_____

Engage in Next Action Thinking

Create a monitoring system to become conscious of your use of cause-effect language and to develop new habits of reporting your feelings, engaging in dialogue, and making requests. Specify what actions you will take and by what date you will take those actions.

_____

_____

_____

_____

_____

_____

_____

_____

CHAPTER 17

Stand Up for Your Point of View

Speak your mind, even if your voice shakes.

—Bumper sticker

What enables choices is the courage of our own voice. And that voice takes place through what we do, what we say, and how we show up.

—Richard Leider

> **My assumptions: Educational leaders increase their inter-personal influence and ability to produce the results they desire when they clearly, succinctly, and persistently express their observations, intentions, and assumptions in the spirit of dialogue.**

"Standing up" in conversations means expressing the unique perspective and assumptions that each of us add to a discussion and doing so persistently over time. Standing up means bringing the passion of your values, purpose, and intentions; the uniqueness of your observations; and the intellectual clarity of your assumptions to all of your interactions. It also means having confidence and pride in your point of view and the courage to speak your mind in important situations. Taking a stand is a significant way that leaders change the conversation in ways that perturb systems, provoke important professional learning, and produce the results they seek.

When leaders present new ideas or initiate professional learning, they traditionally do so in relatively standard ways—they offer research or other forms of information through presentations, books, or articles; they ask questions; and they sometimes engage others in activities such as small-group discussion to consider or apply what has been presented. I am proposing an alternative way of stimulating professional learning that is appropriate to many everyday settings: Whenever appropriate, leaders state their observations in a descriptive, nonjudgmental way; they explain their intentions regarding the subject and the assumptions that underlie them; and they ask for what they want. Along the way, they engage in dialogue to bring depth and clarity to the conversation.

> Those people who experience the greatest joy offer to the world their distinctiveness.
>
> —George Land &
> Beth Jarman

Stating our observations in descriptive, nonjudgmental terms may seem like a relatively easy thing to do, but it can be one of the most challenging skills presented in this book. Most of us have deeply ingrained habits of perception and speech that lead us to infer, assume, and speculate rather than simply note what our senses reveal to us.

For the most part, stating an observation means saying what we see and hear. It may also include a statement of what we are thinking or feeling, again reported in a nonjudgmental, factual manner. It is like holding up a mirror that reveals to others what we note around us or making ourselves transparent so our thoughts and feelings are known to those with whom we interact. We do not, however, speculate or infer meaning beyond the observation.

> Individuals face the same challenge as organizations. They must find what they deeply care about, what gives their life passionate meaning and then harness those things to a compelling purpose. Each of us has been gifted with our own remarkable way of expressing our humanity.
>
> —George Land &
> Beth Jarman

Here are two examples: Instead of saying "It's clear you really dislike what I just said," we might say, "I noticed that while I was speaking you turned your body to the side and closed your eyes." In making ourselves transparent, we might simply say "I am feeling really frustrated at the moment" or "I'm finding myself thinking that we have begun the process of solving a problem that we haven't yet clearly defined."

An advantage of stating observations over drawing inferences is that others are less likely to become defensive, particularly when we in turn invite the expression of their observations for the purpose of developing shared understanding. The person may respond, "Thanks for pointing that out and giving me the opportunity to say how I see things." At other times, our observations may simply be ignored. At still other times, in spite of our best efforts to the contrary, our observations may provoke defensiveness and anger. That is a time to practice the committed listening skills discussed in Chapter 13. It may be necessary to repeat this cycle—stating observations and assumptions, making requests, engaging in dialogue, listening in a committed way—with patience and persistence over many months before our views begin to gain traction.

> Live as if your life makes a difference. Offer your unique talents to realize the future purpose and possibilities of making the world a better place—in every situation.
>
> —George Land & Beth Jarman

For many of us, a lack of practice in clarifying and stating our observations and assumptions makes this unfamiliar and difficult. Exposing our perspective and thinking to the scrutiny of others can be intellectually demanding and even threatening. One way we avoid putting our views on the line is to quote experts as a method of stating our thoughts without taking the risk of claiming them as our own. We may say, for instance, "Michael Fullan thinks improvement efforts are often fragmented and incoherent" rather than "From my perspective, our improvement efforts are fragmented and incoherent." While we always want to credit others for their original ideas and the words they have written, there comes a point in our journey to effectiveness at which we own the idea, express it in our own unique way, and apply it concretely to the matter at hand. A direct expression of our views, I believe, is more persuasive than obliquely made assertions expressed through the words of others.

EXAMINE YOUR ASSUMPTIONS

Write your assumptions regarding the value of clarifying and standing up for one's views, stating them as succinctly and powerfully as possible. For instance, you may believe "Strongly and clearly expressing my views is a waste of time and risky because no one takes them seriously and they may offend people who can affect my job and career." Share your assumptions with colleagues in the spirit of dialogue.

_____

_____

_____

_____

_____

_____

_____

DEEPEN YOUR UNDERSTANDING

Describe times when you stood up for what you believed and the consequences of your actions. Discuss ways that you might have been more effective in expressing your views.

_____

_____

_____

_____

_____

_____

_____

_____

_____

ENGAGE IN NEXT ACTION THINKING

Identify situations in which standing up for your point of view will help you and others create desired results. Specify with whom and by when you will do so.

_____

_____

_____

_____

_____

_____

_____

_____

_____

PART III

Transformation Through Professional Learning and Doing

Leaders are perpetual learners. . . . Learning is the essential fuel for the leader, the source of high-octane energy that keeps up the momentum by continually sparking new understanding, new ideas, and new challenges.

—Warren Bennis & Burt Nanus

The greatest creative challenge is not only to do something different, but to be something different. The most creative act is the modeling of your own life. . . . Those people who experience the greatest joy offer to the world their distinctiveness.

—George Land & Beth Jarman

In far too many classrooms, students miss out on essential knowledge and skills because of poor-quality or mediocre teaching. In addition, far too many students lack meaningful relationships with their peers and with adults. These students leave their K–12 education with a diminished sense of possibilities for their lives.

A related problem is that most teachers experience mind-numbing and demeaning professional development that creates dependency. Even relatively well-executed "pull-out" staff development seldom affects a school's culture, extends to the classroom, or is sustained over enough time to affect instructional practice. In most schools, a large gap exists between what is known about professional learning that affects teaching and improves student achievement and the professional development that teachers and principals regularly experience.

The solution to these problems, I believe, is high-quality, school-based professional learning and collaborative work that affects all teachers virtually every day. Such learning will deepen understanding, transform beliefs and assumptions to support new practices, and provide a continuous stream of powerful goal-focused actions that keeps improvements on track.

Because a great deal has been written about quality professional learning,* the concluding chapters in this book focus on assisting you in developing a clear, compelling point of view about effective professional development to inform the types of conversations described in this book.

As you will see in the chapters that follow, the most powerful forms of professional development:

- Are sustained, focus relentlessly on improving student learning, and provide personalized in-school and in-classroom assistance to teachers;
- Enable schools to focus their efforts on a small number of student-learning goals and use resources more effectively to alter classroom practice;
- Are both practical and intellectually rigorous and produce complex, intelligent behavior that is the hallmark of skillful teaching and leadership;
- Deepen teachers' content knowledge, expand their repertoire of instructional strategies, and connect them to one another in sustained, interdependent ways;
- Engage teachers virtually every day with their colleagues in examining their students' work, considering data, improving their lessons, deepening their understanding of what they teach, and expanding the number of methods available to teach that content successfully to all students;
- Create schools in which teachers feel emotionally connected to a larger, compelling purpose and to each other in a professional community; and
- Energize schools to pull resources toward them that support their continuous improvement to and use the best available knowledge and skills within and around them.

---

*Visit www.nsdc.org to study the National Staff Development Council's Standards for Staff Development, NSDC's Code of Ethics, *Designing Powerful Professional Development for Teachers and Principals,* by Dennis Sparks (NSDC, 2002), and many other publications that are available for free downloading.

The professional development described in Part III—combined with the professional learning promoted by the type of interpersonal connections advocated in this book—can strengthen the quality of teaching in every classroom and continuously improve student learning. Those are the criteria against which results-focused leadership will ultimately be judged.

CHAPTER 18

Design Powerful Professional Learning for All Educators

[T]eachers who know a lot about teaching and learning and who work in environments that allow them to know students well are the critical elements of successful learning.

—Linda Darling-Hammond

Today, people believe that professional development should be targeted and directly related to teachers' practice. It should be site-based and long-term. It should be ongoing—part of a teacher's work week, not something that's tacked on. And it should be curriculum-based, to the extent possible, so that it helps teachers help their students master the curriculum at a higher level.

—James Stigler

My assumptions: Quality professional development focuses on improving the learning of all students, deepens understanding of what is taught and of the most powerful ways of teaching it, affects educators' beliefs about teaching and learning, and produces a coherent stream of actions that continuously improve teaching, learning, and leadership. The most powerful forms of professional learning are embedded in teachers' daily work, address the core tasks of teaching, and support teachers in forming productive relationships with colleagues and students.

T he welfare of young people and the future of our nation require that all students have quality teaching each day and are surrounded by supportive relationships with peers and adults. From my perspective, that requires that all teachers participate in team-focused professional learning as part of their daily work.

The most effective professional development has a sustained focus on achieving student-learning goals derived from clear and high expectations for all students. Quality teaching and skillful leadership are manifestations of complex, intelligent behavior, behavior that is refined by continuous, intellectually rigorous professional learning.

> Team learning is vital because teams, not individuals, are the fundamental learning unit in modern organization.
>
> —Peter Senge

Therefore, the most powerful forms of professional development make cognitive demands on teachers and administrators and require the progressive use of increasingly higher-level intellectual skills. That means quality professional learning results from the sustained study of research and other professional literature, the analysis of school and classroom data and other evidence of student performance, and the exchange of professional judgments.

> There is plenty of evidence around that, when teachers know their content and know how to teach it at high levels to all students, "teaching to the test" fades into the background of everyday instruction and learning.
>
> —Anne Lewis

The professional learning advocated here skillfully blends the abstract and intellectual with the concrete and immediately useful. Such learning asks teachers to stand back to look at things from a broader perspective, to dig deeply into the consequences of their actions, and to act in ways that will make a significant difference in the learning of their students.

Powerful professional development hones in on the content knowledge and instructional processes that most affect student learning. When teachers study the subjects they teach and expand their repertoire of strategies to teach that content, they will improve their teaching and student learning. That claim is particularly true, I believe, given the complex instructional challenges of classrooms with increasingly diverse students. Teachers' study of content knowledge and teaching methods is aided when teachers consider how students learn a particular subject and the best ways of teaching that subject (an understanding that some experts call pedagogical content knowledge).

Because learning has a strong social component and because the synergy that comes from group problem solving often leads to innovative solutions, the most powerful forms of professional development are centered on teams within schools. Team meetings occur for the most part during the school day because they are an important part of teachers' work responsibilities and benefit from the participation of all teachers, a goal that is difficult to achieve after school and during the summer.

> In all subjects, especially math and science, research indicates that many teachers do not understand the substance well enough to teach concepts, problem formulation and solving, and other higher-order thinking skills now expected as learning outcomes.
>
> —National Institute on Educational Governance, Finance, Policy Making, and Management

The quality of relationships among adults in schools is a predictor of student learning, particularly in schools that are most challenged by the social ills of poverty and racism. High levels of trust, respectful and honest exchanges of views, and a shared commitment to worthwhile goals are some of the most important characteristics of these relationships. Without such relationships, few schools will take full advantage of available resources.

> To last and to have lasting impact, professional development programs would do well to encourage informed debate and healthy unrest among their participants.
>
> —Mary Ann Smith

When professional development is well planned and well executed:

- Teachers hold challenging goals for all students and continuously reflect on various forms of evidence regarding student learning.
- Teachers share planning and learning time that promotes meaningful collaboration. Teachers participate in one or more learning teams within which they are mutually accountable for student learning within the broad context of a professional learning community.
- The organization's culture fosters mutual respect, high levels of trust, and innovative solutions to problems. Teachers experience the emotional and social support such communities provide.

- Teachers are intellectually stimulated by their work. Their productive interactions with peers and with various external providers (for instance, district offices, universities, intermediate service agencies, consultants) deepen their understanding of the content they teach, broaden the range of instructional strategies they bring to their classrooms, and improve relationships with students.
- Methods such as classroom coaching, demonstration lessons, lesson study, the examination of student work, and action research ground professional learning in daily practice and its influence on student learning.
- Teachers pursue professional learning through courses, institutes, and conferences when it is important for the achievement of school goals. They may also participate in cross-school or district networks that strengthen content knowledge and pedagogy.

The *National Staff Development Council's Standards for Staff Development*, the Council's Code of Ethics, and other professional literature are available at www.nsdc.org and can provide materials that can deepen your understanding of these approaches.

Virtually every school can make significant progress in creating such forms of professional learning in a single school year. It is critically important, I believe, that school and district leaders declare high-quality professional learning of the type described here a priority goal within their circle of influence and set about achieving it with the sense of urgency it deserves. Students pass through our schools only once, and they will be the ultimate beneficiaries of the quality teaching such professional learning can produce in every classroom.

EXAMINE YOUR ASSUMPTIONS

Write your assumptions regarding the attributes of quality professional learning. For instance, you may believe "Achieving the kind of professional development described in this chapter will take many years, and the only viable option is to make certain that teacher workshops are relevant to school goals and enjoyed by teachers." Share your assumptions with colleagues in the spirit of dialogue.

_____

_____

_____

_____

_____

_____

DEEPEN YOUR UNDERSTANDING

Describe in detail your long-term goals for the type of professional development you want for all teachers in your school or school system. Discuss which aspects of your vision can be realized in the next school year if the school or district leadership team acts with urgency.

_____

_____

_____

_____

_____

ENGAGE IN NEXT ACTION THINKING

Specify actions that will be taken to make your vision a reality, who will take them, and by what date you will take those actions.

_____

_____

_____

_____

_____

_____

CHAPTER 19

Match Professional Development Goals and Methods With Student Outcomes

The notes of the lecturer are passed to the notes of the listener—without going through the mind of either.

—Mortimer Adler

To create and sustain for children the conditions for productive growth without those conditions existing for educators is virtually impossible.

—Seymour Sarason

> **My assumptions: Professional development is most effective when to a large extent its goals and methods match the goals and methods teachers are expected to use with their students. The qualities of mind and relationships we wish to create for students depend on creating those same qualities of mind and relationships for their teachers and principals.**

Far too often, educators experience professional development whose intention and form are disconnected from the recommendations it makes for student learning. For example, teachers sit passively while experts lecture them on the importance of active learning in their classrooms. Or they receive a cursory presentation that skims across the surface of ways to promote students' deep understanding of subject matter. Or they are told to create caring communities within their classrooms while working in schools whose cultures and daily schedules are barriers from them knowing and trusting one another.

I see a critical link between the goals and methods advocated for students and the kinds of professional learning and relationships essential in creating schools in which youngsters and adults experience success.

To prepare for this chapter, I thumbed through several journals from the past few years to find articles that advocated particular student outcomes and instructional approaches for achieving them. The September 2003 issue of *Educational Leadership* provided a rich resource to illustrate my point with a collection of articles on "Building Classroom Relationships."

In that issue, Robert Marzano and Jane Marzano tell their readers that relationships within schools cannot be left to chance; Steven Wolk recommends engaged learning and caring teacher-student relationships and classrooms that are interesting, intellectual, creative, communal, and purposeful; Jonathan Erwin describes the power of warm, trusting human relationships; Richard Strong, Harvey Silver, Matthew Perini, and Greg Tuculescu discuss the value of mastery, understanding, self-expression, and relationships; and Dan Hoffman and Barbara Levak emphasize the importance of knowing, trusting, empowering, connecting with, and honoring all students.

> In order to offer students the kinds of experiences that reformers want them to have, teachers need to immerse themselves in similar experiences.
>
> —Mary Ann Smith

Also in this issue, Ernest Mendes recalls from his teaching experience that "Every student with whom I consciously made an effort to establish a rapport or a caring relationship demonstrated dramatic changes in behavior, effort, and performance." Jane Katch writes that she wants her students to "develop empathy, look at a situation from another person's point of view, and form a classroom in which each child is a valued member."

> I don't believe in teacher-proof materials. If a teacher is not a critical thinker, how can we expect our kids to be critical thinkers?
>
> —Diana Lam

If we change words such as *student* or *child* to *teacher* and the location from *classroom* to *school*, we are describing the attributes of professional development and a collaborative work environment that I believe would immensely improve the quality of teaching and student learning. In such schools, caring, respectful, and energizing professional and personal relationships among adults would be cultivated, every person would feel valued, teachers' intellectual and creative capacities would be nurtured, sustained learning would lead to mastery of complex professional skills that would be applied in adult contexts as well as the classroom, and teachers would feel empowered rather than resigned or dependent.

> If teachers decide that their goals for students' learning include understanding, then professional development programs should give them time to think about what they mean by "understanding" and how they engage student in the process of understanding.
>
> —Vicki Jacobs

Schools with these qualities would not only be outstanding places for students, but would attract, retain, and continuously renew talented teachers. Our goal, then, as educational leaders is to create a system of schools each of which would be such an outstanding place for students and adults alike that we would eagerly participate in them even if we did not know in advance whether we would be a student, a teacher, or an administrator nor how long we would remain in those roles. What a wonderful school that would be for everyone who had the good fortune to spend time within it!

EXAMINE YOUR ASSUMPTIONS

Write your assumptions regarding the value of aligning goals and methods advocated for students with those for educators, stating them as succinctly and powerfully as possible. For instance, you may believe "Because teachers are professionals, intellectual stimulation and participation in a strong caring community are unnecessary for them to develop those qualities in their students." Share your assumptions with colleagues in the spirit of dialogue.

_____

_____

_____

_____

_____

_____

_____

DEEPEN YOUR UNDERSTANDING

Describe in detail the broad cognitive, behavioral, and affective outcomes your school or school system seeks to develop in students and the characteristics of the environment in which they would learn each day. Do the same for teachers and administrators. Discuss the alignment between these two sets of qualities.

_____

_____

_____

_____

_____

_____

_____

ENGAGE IN NEXT ACTION THINKING

Determine what actions will be taken to align the goals and methods of adult learning and interaction with those intended for students. Specify who will take those actions and by what date.

_____

_____

_____

_____

_____

_____

_____

REFERENCE

Scherer, M. (Ed.). (2003). Building classroom relationships. *Educational Leadership, 61*(1).

CHAPTER 20

Bridge the Knowing-Doing Gap

What matters to us does not suffer from lack of knowledge or skills. To say we need more skills before we can do anything is usually an excuse.

—Peter Block

The development of real knowledge requires intentional activity. If you wait to know something before you do something, likely neither will happen.

—David Allen

> **My assumptions: Most educators know more about effective practice than they regularly employ in their work. The consistent use of what is already known would lead to significant improvements in leadership, teaching, and learning. Learning by doing is an important and underused method of reducing the knowing-doing gap.**

Most of us know more about teaching, leadership, and ways to improve schools than our actions demonstrate. While that does not mean that there are not important things for us to learn, I believe leadership, teaching, and learning will get quite a bit better when educators more consistently apply what they already know.

I've joked over the years that I've wanted to declare an official year of "no professional learning." During that year, anyone caught learning in the traditional ways would be publicly chastised so that everyone's efforts would be focused on doing what he or she already knows, reflecting on the effectiveness of those actions, and on applying the new learning that would emerge from that action. Sometimes it even seems as if staff development–oriented educators have a default mechanism that moves them toward "head learning" whenever they are faced with a new problem. And because that learning often reveals other gaps in academic knowledge, they engage in even more such learning in the quest for "complete understanding," which further postpones action and the important learning such action can generate.

> Our problem is not a lack of tools. We have more tools than we need, many of them we will never use, so why keep enlarging the workshop instead of producing something we are proud of?
>
> —Peter Block

Jeffrey Pfeffer and Robert Sutton (2000) address this issue in *The Knowing-Doing Gap: How Smart Companies Turn Knowledge into Action.* "[O]ne of the great mysteries in organizational management," they write, is "why knowledge of what needs to be done frequently fails to result in action or behavior consistent with that knowledge. We came to call this the *knowing-doing problem*" (p. 4). They note that "... research demonstrates that the success of most interventions designed to improve organizational performance depends largely on implementing what is already known rather than from adopting new or previously unknown ways of doing things" (p. 14).

> We will pay an expert hundreds of dollars an hour for legal, financial, or psychotherapeutic advice, but we're unwilling to pay ourselves the courtesy of trusting that our own instincts and knowledge can guide us to the successful completion of our creative projects. Too often we doubt that we have the right information, ideas, and skills. . . .
>
> —Eric Maisel

Pfeffer and Sutton list numerous organizational processes that substitute for implementing new practices: making a decision to do something as if the decision itself were sufficient to bring about the change, writing a mission statement, engaging in planning, preparing written documents, making presentations and talking "smart" about the change, and so on. While each of these activities may have value, when they are viewed as sufficient in and of themselves, they become sources of the knowing-doing gap, the authors claim.

Here are some additional ideas from the book that have important implications for school leaders:

- "[O]ne of the most important insights from our research is that knowledge that is actually implemented is much more likely to be acquired from learning by doing than from learning by reading, listening, or even thinking" (pp. 5–6).
- "Great companies get remarkable performance from ordinary people" (p. 6).
- "Attempting to copy [from other organizations] just *what* is done—the explicit practices and policies—without holding the underlying philosophy is at once a more difficult task and an approach that is less likely to be successful" (p. 24).
- "[A]t one level, the answer to the knowing-doing problem is deceptively simple: Embed more of the process of acquiring new knowledge in the actual doing of the task and less in formal training programs that are frequently ineffective" (p. 27).
- The "mystique of complexity" employs jargon as a form of status seeking. "The use of complex language hampers implementation even more, however, when leaders or managers don't really understand the meaning of the language they are using and its implications for action. It is hard enough to explain what a complex idea means for action when you understand it and others don't. It is impossible when you use terms that sound impressive but you don't really understand what they mean" (p. 52).

> That individuals, organizations, and countries are not doing very well at converting knowledge to practice is well known in the United States.
>
> —Gerald Nadler & Shozo Hibino

- "You're likely to find talk substituting for action when no follow-up is done to ensure that what was said is actually done; people forget that merely making a decision doesn't change anything; planning, meetings, and report writing become defined as 'action' that is valuable in its own right, even if it has no effect on what people actually do . . . ; complex language, ideas, processes, and structures are thought to be better than simple ones; there is a belief that managers are people who talk and others do; and

> If we are waiting for more knowledge, more skills, more support from the world around us, we are waiting too long. . . . We think there is a right way, that someone else knows what it is, and that it is our job to figure it out. And the world conspires with this illusion, for it wants to sell us an answer.
>
> —Peter Block

internal status comes from talking a lot, interrupting, and being critical of others' ideas" (p. 54).

- "[O]rganizations that were better at learning and translating knowledge into action understood the virtue of simple language, simple structures, simple concepts, and the power of common sense, which is remarkably uncommon in its application" (p. 59).
- "People and the organizations in which they work are often trapped by implicit theories of behavior that guide their decisions and actions. Because the theories are not surfaced or conscious, they can't be refuted with data or logic. In fact, people may not even be conscious of how the theories are directing their behavior. . . . [O]ne of the most powerful interventions we have uncovered to free people from the unconscious power of implicit theory: making people think carefully about the assumptions implicit in the practices and interventions they are advocating. . . . By bringing to the surface assumptions that are otherwise unconscious, interventions and decisions become much more mindful and incorporate what people know" (pp. 91–92).

> People learn best through active involvement and through thinking about becoming articulate about what they have learned.
>
> —Ann Lieberman

Clarity of thought and speech, embedding learning in doing, taking action with accountability, examining our own implicit assumptions and encouraging others to do the same—those are familiar themes of this book.

EXAMINE YOUR ASSUMPTIONS

Write your assumptions regarding the knowing-doing gap, stating them as succinctly and powerfully as possible. For instance, you may believe "A lack of knowledge and skill is the real problem in improving teaching and learning, not the implementation of what is already known." Share your assumptions with colleagues in the spirit of dialogue.

_____

_____

_____

_____

_____

DEEPEN YOUR UNDERSTANDING

Describe ways that you have learned by engaging in action and reflecting on the effects of that action. In addition, discuss ways you have assisted others in considering "the assumptions implicit in the practices and interventions" they regularly employ.

_____

_____

_____

_____

_____

_____

ENGAGE IN NEXT ACTION THINKING

Specify ways in which you will reduce the knowing-doing gap for yourself and for your organization, the actions that will be taken as a result of this discussion, who will take them, and by what date.

_____

_____

_____

_____

_____

_____

_____

REFERENCES

Pfeffer, J., & Sutton, R. (2000). *The knowing-doing gap: How smart companies turn knowledge into action.* Boston: Harvard Business School Press.

CHAPTER 21

Appeal to the Heart as Well as the Head

The fallacy of rationalism is the assumption that the social world can be altered by logical argument. The problem, as George Bernard Shaw observed, is that "reformers have the idea that change can be achieved by brute sanity."

—Michael Fullan

People get the courage to try new things not because they are convinced to do so by a wealth of analytical evidence but because they feel something viscerally.

—Gary Hamel

> **My assumptions: Initiating and maintaining the momentum of significant change requires experiences that appeal to the heart as well as the head. Intellectual engagement alone is usually insufficient to produce such changes.**

"People change what they do less because they are given analysis that shifts their *thinking* than because they are shown a truth that influences their *feelings*," John Kotter and Dan Cohen argue in *The Heart of Change: Real-Life Stories of How People Change Their Organizations* (2002, p. 1). Emotion underlies lasting change, Kotter and Cohen believe, and that emotion is generated more by vivid stories and images—even images that disturb rather than uplift—than it is by research and analysis that provide logical reasons for change. Things that people can see, hear, and touch generate energy that is often lacking from more formal intellectual processes, Kotter and

Cohen say. This emotion provides the passion and commitment that overcomes complacency and inertia and that enables individuals to change often difficult-to-break habits.

Pam Robbins, a consultant to schools, provides an example of such a process. In a letter to me, she wrote:

> [I]t's not a matter of having better information. . . . It's a matter of moral imagination, a wisdom of the heart.
>
> —Paul Ray & Sherry Ruth Anderson

Recently, I had the opportunity to represent NSDC in an on-site consultation with Los Angeles Unified School District D. The superintendent, Ronni Ephraim who had recently come to District D, met with all the administrators one morning to update them on the "State of the District." During the course of her remarks, she commended two administrators who had handled a very tragic situation—the loss of an elementary student in a car accident—with empathy, care and sensitivity.

As she continued with her remarks, Ephraim said that she wanted to leave the group with a "visual reminder" of the challenges facing every school. At that point, she asked two staff members to "unroll" a list of students who had not met proficiency in English language arts. The list was one-eighth of a mile long! It stretched four times across the ballroom in which we were seated. The group sat silently, in awe. The superintendent urged the audience not to think of the list as a "group" of students, but rather as a series of individuals—each with their own needs, hopes, dreams, and aspirations. Ephraim added that a careful examination of the list would yield an awareness that many of the names represented African-American and Latino students. She noted that many of the same names could be found on the lists of non-proficient students in other disciplines as well.

> Many so-called learning experiences don't provide opportunities for real thinking. Meetings are just thinly veiled attempts to persuade others . . . to agree with the teacher's . . . conclusions. Real thinking occurs only when everyone is engaged in exploring differing viewpoints.
>
> —Susan Scott

I was deeply moved by this experience and observed that most of the administrators sitting around me were as well. Following the superintendent's remarks, I met with middle and high school principals. Our "visual reminder" became the foundation for examining the notion that schools that support the continuing development of students also support the continuing development of those who work with those students, as we addressed the topic of using meetings as learning-focused, capacity-building opportunities.

Research, data, and analysis have a role to play in improving teaching and learning. But without stories, images, and experiences that touch the heart, it is difficult to break through complacency and inertia to the sources of energy that are essential to sustained collaborative work, professional learning, and the development of new habits.

EXAMINE YOUR ASSUMPTIONS

Write your assumptions regarding the significance of emotion generated through vivid stories, images, and experiences, stating them as succinctly and powerfully as possible. For instance, you may believe "The most persuasive way to initiate and sustain change is by providing teachers and administrators with reports that describe the very best scientifically based research." Share your assumptions with colleagues in the spirit of dialogue.

_____

_____

_____

_____

_____

_____

DEEPEN YOUR UNDERSTANDING

Provide examples from your personal and professional lives when you were motivated to action by emotionally compelling stories, images, or experiences. Discuss ways that you could create such images, stories, and experiences to motivate and sustain change in your setting.

_____

_____

_____

_____

_____

_____

ENGAGE IN NEXT ACTION THINKING

Specify what actions will be taken to use images, stories, and experiences to motivate and sustain change, who will take them, and by what date.

_____

_____

_____

_____

_____

_____

REFERENCE

Kotter, J., & Cohen, D. (2002). *The heart of change: Real-life stories of how people change their organizations.* Boston: Harvard Business School Press.

CHAPTER 22

Amplify Positive Deviance in Schools

The traditional model for social and organization change doesn't work. It never has. You can't bring permanent solutions in from outside.

—Jerry Sternin

Knowingly or not, commercial publishers, staff development consultants and trainers, and district and state officials have formed an alliance that has repeatedly diminished the ability of local educators to think critically and responsibly. The marketing of answers for schools has kept schools habitually dependent on external authorities. . . . Members of the local school community are made to believe, or have internalized the belief, that educational change is the province of others . . . External programs, materials, consultants, and research can and should be considered and possibly used when a school makes it own decisions, but a school should look first for resources within.

—Carl Glickman

> **My assumptions: The quality of teaching and student learning can be significantly improved with the professional expertise that already resides within virtually all schools. Leadership practices and school cultures that "amplify positive deviance" are a primary means by which schools can continuously improve teaching and learning, demonstrate deep appreciation for the talents of staff members, and retain competent teachers.**

In a common approach to school reform, researchers identify "best practices," which they disseminate through publications and conferences. In turn, school systems prescribe them to teachers who are monitored carefully for compliance. Little regard is shown for the intelligence and capacities that already reside within schools. Another far less frequently applied approach taps the "positive deviance" that exists in schools and amplifies it across classrooms.

> Even though expert guidance is occasionally helpful, the people involved in a specific situation generally know more about it than outside experts.
>
> —Gerald Nadler & Shozo Hibino

"Positive deviants," Jerry Sternin told me in a Winter 2004 *JSD* interview, "are people whose behavior and practices produce solutions to problems that others in the group who have access to exactly the same resources have not been able to solve. We want to identify these people because they provide demonstrable evidence that solutions to the problem already exist within the community" (p. 46).

Sternin's view is that within virtually every school there are individuals whose behavior enables them to get better-than-average results and that these individuals have discovered pathways to success for the rest of the group. That's contrary to a particularly potent and usually unquestioned assumption in education—and perhaps in other fields as well—that solutions to problems must come from the outside because

> Most current reforms, rather than seeking to make teachers into co-developers, simply call for them to carry out experts' prescriptions.
>
> —Robert Evans

those on the inside either don't know enough to improve things or don't have the will to do the hard work of change. That view is particularly strong regarding schools that have a history of low performance.

In the *JSD* interview, I asked Sternin to elaborate on his views regarding outside assistance. "People learn best," he said, "when they discover things for themselves. Knowledge is usually insufficient to change behavior. It is our own discoveries that change behavior. A basic belief of the Positive Deviance Approach is that when someone from the outside provides the solution, those to whom it is directed may not believe it and do not have an investment in it" (p. 48).

Sternin added: "It's natural for people to resist when someone tells them what to do. That's part of human nature. It's like the human immune system's rejection of anything it senses as foreign. It's the same thing as the psychological and emotional levels when an external solution is imposed on us. When the solution comes from within the system, the immune response isn't activated" (p. 48).

The Positive Deviance Approach has six steps: define, determine, discover, design, discern, and disseminate "The group begins its work by defining the problem and describing what success would look like—which is the inverse of the problem statement" Sternin said. "Next, the group determines if there are individuals who have already achieved success. If there are such people, they are the positive deviants. Next, the group discovers the uncommon but demonstrably successful behaviors and practices used by the positive deviants to solve the problem. And finally, the group designs an intervention which enables its members to practice those demonstrably successful but uncommonly applied practices. The process is beautifully simple because its strength lies in the solutions that are discovered and owned by people in the community" (p. 49). The final two steps are discerning the effectiveness of the intervention and sharing the successful intervention with a wider audience.

> We should attach the most importance to improving our teaching methods. Most students are taught by an average teacher, implementing the average method. If we can find a way to make the average method a little bit better, that's going to have a big effect.
>
> —James Stigler

The physical presence of the positive deviant in the affected community is a significant aspect of the inquiry process. But that presence alone is usually insufficient. For instance, a principal who has heard about positive deviance may invite a teacher who has consistently produced higher reading-test scores to tell her peers how she does it. What often occurs, however, is that the faculty resists and the teacher identified by the principal may even feel shunned by her colleagues.

Sternin explains it this way: "The Positive Deviance Approach requires that community members find the positive deviants within their own community. The community is self-defined and its members always share the same resource base. . . . That's important, and it's a critical distinction between a best-practices approach and positive deviance" (p. 50).

> The very best thing you can do for a superintendent . . . is not to give him more money, more buildings, or a better contract. Instead, give him a tool to make his average teachers just a little bit better, and you'll see a vastly greater impact across the district than any model school or blue-ribbon program will ever bring.
>
> —Superintendent, as quoted by Peter Temes

While the Positive Deviance Approach honors and appreciates the people who engage in it, it may be difficult for traditional "experts" to implement. "Positive deviance," Sternin told me, "is a very empowering approach, but it's one that individuals with lots of degrees on their walls may find it difficult to implement. Positive deviance inquires into what's working and how it can be built upon to solve very difficult problems. It requires that experts relinquish their power and believe that solutions already reside within the system. Our role is to help people discover their answers" (p. 51).

Schools that systematically identify, deeply appreciate, and spread the outstanding practices that already exist within them will also be more effective in using external sources of knowledge, I believe. And schools whose cultures are contrary to such methods will derive few lasting benefits from most externally imposed "solutions." Amplifying positive deviance is a promising, nonprescriptive approach for schools that see value in its premises and are ready to empower teachers through its inquiry process.

> Ultimately, no amount of outside intervention can produce the motivation and specificity of best solutions for every setting.
>
> —Michael Fullan

EXAMINE YOUR ASSUMPTIONS

Write your assumptions about amplifying positive deviance, stating them as succinctly and powerfully as possible. For instance, you may believe "The Positive Deviance Approach cannot work in my setting because teachers have no desire to learn from one another and positive deviant teachers are often ostracized by their peers." Invite others to share their assumptions with you in a spirit of openness to having your views change.

_____

_____

_____

_____

_____

_____

DEEPEN YOUR UNDERSTANDING

Describe in writing or discuss with others the ways in which amplifying positive deviance is the same and different from other types of professional development with which you are familiar. For example, a common approach is for administrators to identify teachers who produce high test scores and ask them to describe their teaching methods at school or district staff development events, a method that does not engage the school community in the process recommended by Jerry Sternin.

_____

_____

_____

_____

_____

_____

ENGAGE IN NEXT ACTION THINKING

Specify what actions you will take to engage the school community in identifying and designing processes to learn from positive deviant teachers and positive deviant schools.

_____

_____

_____

_____

_____

_____

REFERENCE

Sparks, D. (2004). From hunger aid to school reform. An interview with Jerry Sternin. *JSD, 25*(1), pp. 46–51.

CHAPTER 23

Shape School Culture to Improve Teaching and Sustain Competent Teachers

Teacher isolation is so deeply ingrained in the traditional fabric of schools that leaders cannot simply invite teachers to create a collaborative culture. They must identify and implement specific, strategic interventions that help teachers work together rather than alone.

—Richard DuFour

You cannot order people to become cohesive. You cannot order great performance. You have to create the culture and climate that makes it possible. You have to build the bonds of trust.

—Michael Abrashoff

> **My assumptions: Skillful leadership by principals and teachers is essential if quality teaching is to occur in all classrooms. An essential part of such leadership is the creation of a performance-oriented culture that has professional learning and collaboration at its core.**

High-quality professional learning by all teachers is critically important if we want high-quality learning in all classrooms and if we want to sustain and retain competent teachers throughout their careers.

A primary task of school leaders is the gradual and sustained improvement of teaching in all classrooms by amplifying positive deviance throughout the school, closing the knowing-doing gap, appealing to emotion as well as intel-lect, and infusing external research and expertise when appropriate. Such activity and learning is ultimately based in and stimulated by a high-performance culture, which principals and teacher leaders are responsible for creating.

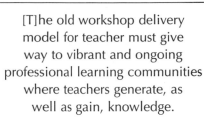

> [T]he old workshop delivery model for teacher must give way to vibrant and ongoing professional learning communities where teachers generate, as well as gain, knowledge.
>
> —Ann Lieberman & Diane Wood

A widely held view of instruc-tional improvement is that good teaching is primarily an individual affair and that principals who view themselves as instructional leaders promote it by interacting one-on-one with each teacher to strengthen his or her efforts in the classroom. The principal is like the hub of a wheel with teachers at the end of each spoke. Communi-cation about instruction moves back and forth along the spokes to the hub but not around the circumference of the wheel.

As other chapters in Part III point out, some of the most important professional learning occurs in daily interactions among teachers when they work together to improve lessons, deepen understanding of the content they teach, analyze student work, examine various types of data on student performance, and solve the myriad of problems they face each day. From this perspective, sustained teacher-to-teacher communication about teaching and learning that is rich and deep in its content and processes is one of the most powerful

> Instead of inviting teachers to watch one another teach, to debate best classroom practices, and to pool resources, the school culture walls them off and parcels out their time. It actually promotes professional distance.
>
> —Mary Ann Smith

and underused sources of professional learning and instructional improvement. A principal's participation is valuable in improving instruction and student learning but it cannot be the primary form of learning-oriented interactions for teachers.

Because culture is the sum total of the beliefs of community members and their interactions, creating such a culture means estab-lishing norms and practices that lead to trust and mutual respect, con-tinuous improvement, team-focused collaboration, clarity of thought, candid expressions of views, and interpersonal accountability for the fulfillment of commitments. In such schools, teachers talk candidly using the type of skills recommended in this book about their views on student learning, teaching, and emotionally charged topics such as race and social class. These conditions seldom occur by chance, and, once they are in place, they are unlikely to be sustained without conscious attention to their maintenance.

> Vital organizations exude health and energy and enthusiasm. Like vital people, they are full of hope and anticipation for things to come.
>
> —Max DePree

School leaders' mental models and the cumulative effect of their actions have a large influence on the cultures within which teachers work. That means professional development for principals and teacher leaders not only prepares them to be instructional leaders who, for instance, know how to assess teaching and learning in classroom "walk-throughs," but also enables them to transform their organizations' cultures. Preparation programs and leadership development efforts are the logical places to teach these skills and provide one-on-one support as they are implemented in the schoolhouse.

> When people share a common vision, they can perform feats that would otherwise be impossible . . . There is something in the human spirit that longs for participation with others, that wants to be involved in a collective endeavor.
>
> —Robert Fritz

The development of transformational leaders is qualitatively different from the information-sharing methods that are the staples of traditional forms of development. Among other things, leaders learn how to engage in the types of conversations recommended in this book for the purpose of deepening understanding, shifting beliefs and assumptions regarding teaching and learning, and promoting next action thinking and interpersonal accountability. These skills are best acquired when leaders personally and consistently *experience* these conversations as they interact with others throughout their development rather than simply *learn about* the attributes of such interactions.

EXAMINE YOUR ASSUMPTIONS

Write your assumptions regarding the significance of school culture in shaping the teaching that occurs within a school and the nature of the professional learning that is essential for school leaders to enable the creation of such schools, stating them as succinctly and powerfully as possible. For instance, you may believe "School culture is deeply ingrained and essentially fixed, and there is little that any-one, including school leaders, can do to alter it." Share your assumptions with colleagues in the spirit of dialogue.

_____

_____

_____

_____

_____

_____

DEEPEN YOUR UNDERSTANDING

Describe from your experience the attributes of a high-performance school culture. For example, reflect on the relationships or practices in your setting that promote excellence and those that are barriers to it. Compare your views with those expressed in this chapter.

_____

_____

_____

_____

_____

_____

ENGAGE IN NEXT ACTION THINKING

Specify the initial actions you will take to shift the culture of your school or school system in the direction of higher performance and by what dates you will take those actions.

_____

_____

_____

_____

_____

_____

_____

CHAPTER 24

Install Next Action Thinking

Our responsibility is not discharged by the announcement of virtuous ends.

—John F. Kennedy

No matter how big and tough a problem may be, get rid of confusion by taking one little step toward solution. Do something.

—George Nordenholt

One of the biggest fears for a creative person is that some brilliant idea will get lost because you didn't write it down and put it in a safe place.

—Twyla Tharp

My assumptions: "Next action thinking" promotes the use of new practices acquired through professional learning, aids in the implementation of plans, and sustains the momentum required to produce valued results. Leaders are more successful when their psychic energy is invested in complex intellectual processes rather than squandered as they worry about whether important tasks have been overlooked by those who have agreed to do them.

"It's not how many ideas your have. It's how many you make happen," a business proclaims in advertisements about its ability to turn "innovation into results." The knowing-doing gap described in Chapter 20 is a manifestation of learning that has simply not been acted upon. Similarly, studies conducted on the effects of strategic planning reveal that less than 10% of well-formulated strategies are successfully implemented. While learning for its own sake and planning for the value of the clarity it produces may be worthy ends in themselves, results are ultimately obtained from actions that we initiate, learn from, and successfully complete.

In this book's Introduction, I noted David Allen's view expressed in *Getting Things Done: The Art of Stress-Free Productivity* (2001) on the power of habitually considering the next action. It bears repeating here: "Over the years, I have noticed an extraordinary shift in energy and productivity whenever individuals and groups installed 'What's the next action?' as a fundamental and consistently asked question" (p. 236). The result, he says, would be that " . . . no meeting or discussion will end, and no interaction cease, without a clear determination of whether or not some action is needed—and, if it is, what it will be, or at least who has responsibility for it" (p. 236). Allen argues that " . . . shifting your focus to something that your mind perceives as a doable, completable task will create a real increase in positive energy, direction, and motivation" (p. 242).

An important aspect of next action thinking and maintaining momentum is making and keeping promises regarding our intentions. Developing agreements about making and keeping promises is important (as discussed more fully in Chapter 15). The options include honoring the agreement, renegotiating it, rescinding it, or breaking the agreement. If an agreement is broken, the protocol may include reporting the breakdown, "cleaning up" the situation in a way that is agreeable to the other person, and recommitting yourself to the agreement, if it is still important to all parties.

Next action thinking is a habit of automatically moving learning and planning into action (more will be said about establishing new habits in Chapter 25). The kinds of professional learning recommended in Part III of this book will be of little consequence if such habits are not established. Once we have habits and procedures for noting, tracking, and completing agreements and norms of interpersonal accountability, we can be fully invested in results-oriented activities rather than tracking whether others have forgotten or overlooked important tasks.

You could employ sophisticated processes and electronic management systems for project planning. Or you could do something as simple as back-of-the-envelope planning that includes writing the goal, the steps to achieve it, and the dates by which those steps will be taken. For particularly complex long-term goals, however, you may want a clear, detailed vision of the preferred end state, a description of the next several actions, and what you expect will be the last step or two required to achieve the goal. Well-laid plans falter because no one was paying attention to the last few essential steps for achieving the goal, what some planners call the "final 2%."

EXAMINE YOUR ASSUMPTIONS

Write your assumptions regarding the significance of next action thinking, stating them as succinctly and powerfully as possible. For instance, you may believe "Next action thinking and the interpersonal accountability it promotes are impractical for busy educators who are juggling too many balls to exercise the type of discipline it requires." Share your assumptions with colleagues in the spirit of dialogue.

_____

_____

_____

_____

_____

_____

DEEPEN YOUR UNDERSTANDING

Discuss professional learning or other forms of professional work that were more effective because actions and lines of accountability were clearly specified. Specify the agreements or procedures that contributed to that effort.

_____

_____

_____

_____

_____

_____

_____

ENGAGE IN NEXT ACTION THINKING

Specify the actions you will take to install the habit of next action thinking and by what dates you will take those actions.

_____

_____

_____

_____

_____

_____

_____

REFERENCE

Allen, D. (2001). *Getting things done: The art of stress-free productivity.* New York: Viking.

CHAPTER 25

Change Habits

[E]ven the most successful leaders can increase their effectiveness by changing certain elements of their behavior.

—Marshall Goldsmith

•

We are what we repeatedly do; excellence, then, is not an act, but a habit.

—Aristotle

> **My assumptions: Leaders' habits affect the results they achieve. Developing new habits usually requires attention, discipline, and feedback on our progress.**

A foundation of human resourcefulness is our ability at any stage of life to develop new habits of thought and behavior that serve our purposes and values. Clarity regarding our values and purpose has limited significance unless that clarity is followed by commitments to specific actions, a sense of accountability for completing those actions, and the development of habits that sustain those changes over time.

A simple system to use when learning a new habit is to establish a measurable goal regarding the new behavior, determine a method to prompt you to use that behavior, promise someone that you will behave in that way to increase your motivation to acquire the new habit, set up a monitoring system to assess progress, and begin practicing the new behavior. This approach can be applied to any of the beliefs or practices recommended in this book. For instance, if you want to decrease or eliminate your use of obligatory language, state that as a goal, tell coworkers of your intention, ask selected individuals to draw attention to such language whenever it is used, and give yourself a daily letter grade or numerical score that reflects your performance.

> Consultants come in and introduce big bold strategies. Everyone learns what is expected, but over time little seems to change. Everyone slowly reverts to how things have always been done, because the small everyday behaviors that really run the show are never addressed. Everyday behaviors are the glue that keeps organizations stuck in the original form no matter how many big bold initiatives are introduced. Yet, hardly anyone focuses on the small stuff.
>
> —Mikela Tarlow

Executive coach Marshall Goldsmith underscores the importance of creating measurable indicators to motivate and assess progress, even for so-called soft goals. He tells a story about his response to his daughter's complaint that he was inattentive to her when he was home during respites from his busy work-related travel schedule. He set a goal to increase the number of days in which he spent at least four hours interacting with his family without the common distractions of TV, movies, or the telephone. The first year he recorded 92 days of "unencumbered interaction," which grew to 135 days over the next four years. (He says that he later recalibrated his goal when his teenage children said they were seeing too much of him.)

Goldsmith also describes a process he calls "feed forward" in which individuals select behaviors they believe will make a positive difference in their lives, ask coworkers for suggestions, listen to their ideas, thank them for their contributions. "No on is allowed to critique suggestions or to bring up the past," he notes (p. 103).

Kerry Patterson, Joseph Grenny, Ron McMillan, and Al Switzer (2002) offer another approach in *Crucial Conversations: Tools for Talking When Stakes Are High.* They suggest four general principles for "turning ideas into action": (1) mastering the content, (2) mastering the related skills, (3) enhancing motivation, and (4) watching for cues to apply the new knowledge and skills. To *master knowledge and skills*, they suggest digging more deeply into an area of particular interest, teaching the skill to someone else, rehearsing with a friend, and selecting a low- or medium-risk situation in which to apply the learning. To *enhance motivation*, they suggest using incentives, celebrating improvements, and making intentions known so others may assist you and provide a disincentive to not following through on the commitment. *Cues to assist in changing habits* include carrying note cards as reminders of the goal, posting small notes around your office or home, and placing large posters or signs to signal your intention to you and to others.

EXAMINE YOUR ASSUMPTIONS

Write your assumptions regarding the significance of developing new habits as a means of creating the results you desire, stating them as succinctly and powerfully as possible. For instance, you may believe "Because behavior is shaped more by organizational culture and structures that surround people than it is by personal habits, leaders will have the greatest impact by focusing on those factors." Share your assumptions with colleagues in the spirit of dialogue.

_____

_____

_____

_____

_____

_____

DEEPEN YOUR UNDERSTANDING

Describe habits that have enabled you to achieve your goals. Discuss the methods you have found most useful in developing new habits of thought and behavior. Consider methods you may have used such as daily reminders posted on a mirror or your desk or a daily diary or log related to changes in diet or exercise habits.

_____

_____

_____

_____

_____

_____

ENGAGE IN NEXT ACTION THINKING

Specify one or more habits you would like to develop, the methods you will use to prompt the new behavior and to monitor your progress, and the date by which you will begin.

_____

_____

_____

_____

_____

_____

REFERENCES

Goldsmith, M. (2004, May). Leave it at the stream. *Fast Company*, 82, 103.

Patterson, K., Grenny, J., McMillan, R., & Switzer, A. (2002). *Crucial conversations: Tools for talking when stakes are high.* New York: McGraw-Hill.

CHAPTER 26

Sustain the Conversation

All learning is social. It is with our peers that we will ultimately find our voice and change our world. It is in community that our lives are transformed. Small groups change the world.

—Peter Block

[A]ll individuals, in conditions of stress, benefit from interpersonal support. Research has shown that the more isolated people are, the more vulnerable they are to stress; support not only makes people feel better, it helps them think better, improving their problem-solving ability.

—Robert Evans

My assumptions: Clear and deeply felt values, a passionate sense of purpose, and meaningful connections with others generate energy to sustain the momentum of continuous improvement. Ongoing recognition of "small wins" maintains motivation and enthusiasm as teachers and administrators learn, create, innovate, and develop new habits.

A story is told in which the composer George Gershwin approaches Maurice Ravel to ask permission to study with him. Ravel responds, "Why would you wish to be a second-rate Ravel when you can be a first-rate Gershwin?" Becoming deeply ourselves—our first-rate selves—is a prerequisite to fulfilling our unique role in creating first-rate organizations. Doing so means gaining clarity about our most deeply felt values and purposes and consistently and courageously representing our point of view in many venues through well-considered words and actions.

Becoming our first-rate selves, however, requires a lifetime of attention and persistence. Our original sense of purpose may wane and our initial enthusiasm diminish. More urgent priorities may claim our attention and take precedence for our time. Even if we are able to stay focused on our goals amidst the press of competing demands, we may become discouraged by setbacks and interpersonal challenges that typically accompany important individual and organizational changes.

> Look around you for people whose conversations are memorable, people who wake you up and provoke your learning—people who are real.
>
> —Susan Scott

This chapter describes numerous ways to sustain the new habits acquired in previous chapters. It describes ways we can deepen our learning, remain in meaningful dialogue, maintain our enthusiasm, and act consistently with our purposes and values to achieve the results most important to us. In addition, I encourage you to invent other ways that draw on your strengths to sustain new habits and extend your learning on these subjects. Here are a few suggestions:

• Stay in tune with your fundamental choices, values, purposes, and intentions and consistently align your actions with them. Clarity regarding values and goals provides energy that fuels our effort in the face of the adversity that almost always accompanies the development of new habits and significant change in individual and organizational practices. Have a laserlike focus on actions that are closely linked to the values and purposes most important to you.

• Apply daily what you have learned in previous chapters about next action thinking and changing habits. For the most part, our professional and personal lives may be viewed as a bundle of habits. What we think about educational matters, the intellectual processes we most commonly use, our manner of speaking, and how we relate to others can be shaped to match our values and purposes. Next action thinking reminds us that the most important action we can take is the next one and that the impetus gained from that action will help shape the one that follows. Taken together, this chain of actions forms our habits and professional practice. No part of our lives is too large or small to benefit from this step-by-step approach to creating the results we desire.

• Have conversations with others in the ways described in this book to focus and sustain your work. High-quality connections with others are a fundamental source of direction and energy for your work and your life. Conversations rich in candor, clarity, purposefulness, committed listening, and dialogue can have a profound effect on individuals and schools.

One way to create interpersonal connections related to your most important goals is to identify individuals or designate a personal "board of directors" to provide emotional and social support and bring diverse perspectives to the creative and improvisational venture that is our lives. Another way some leaders maintain their focus is to seek the services of executive coaches (also called life coaches or results coaches). While these specialists may charge a fee for their services, the benefit of such one-on-one support can be worth the costs. A less-expensive substitute is to ask mentors or friends to serve you in this capacity by practicing the committed listening skills described in Chapter 9 and trusting your ability to find ways to achieve pathways to your goals.

> There was no single defining action, no grand program, no one killer innovation, no solitary lucky break, no wrenching revolution. Good to great comes about by a cumulative process—step by step, action by action, decision by decision, turn by turn of the flywheel—that adds up to sustained and spectacular results.
>
> —Jim Collins

Celebrate progress as well as the accomplishment of your goals. While I emphasized the value of stretch goals and the deep changes they often require in our beliefs and behavior in Chapter 3, motivation for achieving such demanding goals is sustained as we define, achieve, and recognize the accomplishment of each of the subordinate goals that comprise the larger goal. One way to do so is to begin with easy-to-achieve goals—"low-hanging fruit"—to gain a feeling of success and momentum. (However, resist the temptation to stop here thinking that the completion of these low-level activities is the same as accomplishing your larger purpose.) Another process of defining and achieving these smaller goals is the "Swiss cheese method"— poking holes in the larger goal as opportunities present themselves until very little remains to be done. Whatever your approach, recognize and, when appropriate, reward completion of milestones on the journey.

Consciously apply these skills in many settings to expand your influence. Each interaction with others is an opportunity for transformation when approached with a clear sense of what you want to accomplish and the skills you wish to apply in the conversation.

Everything you have learned in this book can be practiced in one-on-one conversations with parents, colleagues, supervisors, and those you supervise; in telephone conversations with parents; as a participant in grade-level, department, school, and district instructional meetings; and in school improvement or professional development committee meetings. These ideas and skills can also be applied when you facilitate meetings or make presentations at faculty meetings, staff development sessions, or parent events.

My hope is that you will use what you have learned in this book to help create schools in which quality teaching occurs in every classroom and teachers and students alike experience success, joy, and satisfaction each day. Such schools are grounded in relationships and intellectual tasks that honor and challenge every member of the community to more fully develop his or her talents to serve both individual and collective purposes. Those are the schools to which I believe we would all happily send our own children.

EXAMINE YOUR ASSUMPTIONS

Write your assumptions regarding the most powerful methods of sustaining energy and enthusiasm for change over time, stating them as succinctly and powerfully as possible. For instance, you may believe "The professional lives of educators are too busy and fragmented these days to expect them to pay attention to their values and purposes, yet alone find time to stay connected with others who share their deepest commitments." Share your assumptions with colleagues in the spirit of dialogue.

_____

_____

_____

_____

_____

_____

Deepen Your Understanding

List individuals you have known or learned about who have lived in alignment with their deepest values and aspirations. Consider individuals whom you have known personally or those you have come to know through biography or works of fiction. Reflect on the methods they used to achieve that alignment. Discuss barriers that you anticipate arising in your life and ways that they may be addressed.

_____

_____

_____

_____

_____

_____

_____

Engage in Next Action Thinking

Specify actions you will take to continue your professional learning and sustain your efforts over many months and years and by what dates you will initiate them.

_____

_____

_____

_____

_____

_____

Index

**CORWIN
PRESS**

The Corwin Press logo—a raven striding across an open book—represents the union of courage and learning. Corwin Press is committed to improving education for all learners by publishing books and other professional development resources for those serving the field of K–12 education. By providing practical, hands-on materials, Corwin Press continues to carry out the promise of its motto: **"Helping Educators Do Their Work Better."**

NSDC's mission is to ensure success for all students by serving as the international network for those who improve schools and by advancing individual and organization development.

NATIONAL ASSOCIATION
OF SECONDARY SCHOOL
PRINCIPALS

The National Association of Secondary School Principals—the preeminent organization and the national voice for middle level and high school principals, assistant principals and aspiring school leaders—provides its members the professional resources to serve as visionary leaders.